Teaching Elementary Grammar with Mentor Texts

Teaching Elementary Grammar with Mentor Texts: Ready to Use Lesson Plans for Grades 3–5 contains detailed grammar lesson plans for teachers in grades three, four, and five.

The lesson plans in this book incorporate the research-based best practices of grammar instruction and apply those practices to the teaching and learning of grammar instruction. They present grammatical concepts in the context of effective writing by using mentor texts. These mentor text examples, which students read from a writer's perspective, deepen students' metacognition of the importance of grammatical concepts and help them see the elements of grammar as tools for strong writing that authors use strategically to make their work as strong as possible.

The book provides elementary school teachers with user-friendly lesson plans that they can easily use to put mentor text-based grammar instruction into action in their classrooms. These lesson plans feature published examples of grammatical concepts from contemporary children's and middle-grade books, activities that help students connect their reading and writing experiences, and reflective activities that facilitate students' metacognition of the importance of grammatical concepts. The thorough plans in this book will help teachers put the best practices of grammar instruction into action in concrete, practitioner-oriented ways.

Sean Ruday (he/him/his) is a professor and program coordinator of English education at Longwood University.

Also Available from Routledge Eye On Education

(https://www.routledge.com/go/routledge-eye-on-education)

Grammar Toolkit Lesson Plans for Middle School: Mentor Text-Based Grammar Lessons for the Middle School English Classroom
Sean Ruday

40 Poems for 40 Weeks: Integrating Meaningful Poetry and Word Ladders into Grades 3–5 Literacy
David L. Harrison and Timothy V. Rasinski

Student-Centered Literacy Assessment in the 6-12 Classroom An Asset-Based Approach
Sean Ruday

Teach This Poem, Volume I: The Natural World
Madeleine Fuchs Holzer and The Academy of American Poets

Close Reading in Elementary School: Bringing Readers and Texts Together, 2nd edition
Diana Sisson and Betsy Sisson

The Antiracist English Language Arts Classroom
Keisha Rembert

The Literacy Coaching Handbook: Working With Teachers to Increase Student Achievement, 2nd edition
Diana Sisson and Betsy Sisson

Teaching Elementary Grammar with Mentor Texts

Ready to Use Lesson Plans for Grades 3–5

Sean Ruday

Routledge
Taylor & Francis Group
NEW YORK AND LONDON

Designed cover image: © Getty Images

First published 2026
by Routledge
605 Third Avenue, New York, NY 10158

and by Routledge
4 Park Square, Milton Park, Abingdon, Oxon, OX14 4RN

Routledge is an imprint of the Taylor & Francis Group, an informa business

© 2026 Sean Ruday

The right of Sean Ruday to be identified as author of this work has been asserted in accordance with sections 77 and 78 of the Copyright, Designs and Patents Act 1988.

All rights reserved. The purchase of this copyright material confers the right on the purchasing institution to photocopy or download pages which bear a copyright line at the bottom of the page. No other parts of this book may be reprinted or reproduced or utilised in any form or by any electronic, mechanical, or other means, now known or hereafter invented, including photocopying and recording, or in any information storage or retrieval system, without permission in writing from the publishers.

Trademark notice: Product or corporate names may be trademarks or registered trademarks, and are used only for identification and explanation without intent to infringe.

ISBN: 978-1-041-00589-6 (hbk)
ISBN: 978-1-041-00587-2 (pbk)
ISBN: 978-1-003-61065-6 (ebk)

DOI: 10.4324/9781003610656

Typeset in Palatino
by KnowledgeWorks Global Ltd.

Access the Support Material: www.routledge.com/9781041005872

Contents

Meet the Author — vii

Introduction: Reimagining Elementary School Grammar Instruction with Mentor Texts — 1

SECTION ONE
Lesson Plans Recommended for the Third-Grade Classroom — 11

Lesson 3.1 Let's Agree: Subject-Verb Agreement — 13

Lesson 3.2 Descriptive Information: Adjectives — 25

Lesson 3.3 The Power of Explanation: Adverbs — 35

Lesson 3.4 Building Sentences: Simple, Compound, and Complex Sentences — 45

Lesson 3.5 In Dialogue: Using Commas and Quotation Marks When Writing Dialogue — 57

SECTION TWO
Lesson Plans Recommended for the Fourth-Grade Classroom — 71

Lesson 4.1 A Big Deal: Capitalization — 73

Lesson 4.2 Showing Conditions: Modal Auxiliaries — 85

Lesson 4.3 Elaborating on Information: Prepositional Phrases — 95

Lesson 4.4 Providing Detail: Relative Clauses — 105

Lesson 4.5 Clear and Powerful Language: Strong Verbs and Specific Nouns — 115

SECTION THREE

Lesson Plans Recommended for the Fifth-Grade Classroom — **127**

Lesson 5.1 Linking and Connecting: Conjunctions — 129

Lesson 5.2 Showing Emotion: Interjections — 140

Lesson 5.3 Pronouns and Clarity: Pronoun-Antecedent Agreement — 149

Lesson 5.4 Beyond the Literal: Figurative Language — 160

Lesson 5.5 Toward Clarity: Using Commas for Clarity — 172

SECTION FOUR

Final Thoughts and Resources — **185**

Conclusion: Putting Mentor Text-Based Grammar Instruction Into Action in Grades Three to Five — 187

Appendix A: Annotated Bibliography of Mentor Texts — 190
Appendix B: Reproducible Graphic Organizers — 197
Appendix C: Lesson Plan Template — 240

Note: Appendices A, B, and C are also available online on this book's webpage on the Routledge site for quick and easy access to these resources

Meet the Author

Sean Ruday (he/him/his) is a professor and program coordinator of English education at Longwood University. He has taught English and language arts in New York, Massachusetts, and Virginia. He holds a BA from Boston College, an MA from New York University, and a PhD from the University of Virginia. Sean is the founding editor of the *Journal of Literacy Innovation*. This is his 19th book with Routledge Eye On Education.

Introduction

Reimagining Elementary School Grammar Instruction with Mentor Texts

When I plan lessons on elementary school grammar instruction, I dive into books! Specifically, I pour through outstanding examples of children's and middle-grade books, finding examples of how the authors of these books use key grammatical concepts in their works. For instance, when recently creating lessons to teach grammatical concepts to elementary school students, I identified published examples of important components of grammar, such as subject-verb agreement, adjectives, prepositional phrases, relative clauses, conjunctions, and interjections. While reading Kareen Getten's (2020) book *When Life Gives You Mangos,* I noted the prepositional phrase "behind the house" in the sentence "I have a secret hideout behind the house" (p. 8). As I marked the example of this grammatical concept in the book with a sticky note, I said to myself, "This published example will help the grammatical concept of prepositional phrases come alive for students. It will show students an authentic example of how a published author uses this concept in a piece of writing." Similarly, when reading the book *Kinda Like Brothers* by Coe Booth (2014), I identified the coordinating conjunction "and" in the sentence "It was still the middle of the night, and I probably hadn't even been asleep for more than an hour" (p. 2). While noting this example, I told myself, "Examples from literature like this one will help students understand how and why writers use coordinating conjunctions."

I share these insights into my planning process to provide insight into how I think about literature-based grammar instruction. When I plan and teach grammar, I incorporate examples from well-written, engaging, published texts that demonstrate strong uses of grammatical concepts. These examples are called mentor texts because they mentor and guide students as they learn about writing and how to apply writing strategies to their own works (Dorfman & Cappelli, 2017), using the features of published texts to help students understand the attributes of strong writing (Ehmann & Gayer, 2009). In the context of grammar instruction, mentor texts help students understand what key grammatical concepts are, how they are used in effective writing, why they are important to strong writing, and how to apply them to their own works. The lesson plans in this book represent this approach and apply it to elementary school grammar instruction: they incorporate mentor texts as part of a strategic and intentional process designed to help students in grades three, four, and five understand, use, and reflect on grammatical concepts that can enhance their own writing, reading, and thinking. In this introductory chapter, we'll explore three concepts related to this book: 1) The best practices of elementary school grammar instruction, 2) this book's approach, and 3) what to expect in this book. Ready? Let's go!

The Best Practices of Elementary School Grammar Instruction

Teaching grammar effectively in elementary school involves breaking away from some traditional practices and rethinking what grammar instruction can look like. Traditionally, grammar has focused on out-of-context worksheets and activities that are presented separately from student writing (Weaver, 1998). These exercises frequently lead to student disengagement (Wotjer, 1998) and have very little impact on student writing (Weaver, 1998). As teachers, this is exactly what we don't want! The disengagement and lack of impact associated with traditional grammar instruction can be especially concerning in the elementary school classroom, where students are beginning to work with and think about grammatical concepts that they'll use in their current literacy practices and well into the future.

Research shows that the most effective grammar instruction makes connections to students' experiences with reading and writing (Smagorinsky, 2018), which is often called teaching grammar in context (Anderson, 2005; Weaver, 1998). The question for us teachers, then, is what is the best way to teach grammar in context? In other words, how can we most effectively teach students about key grammatical concepts, such as those reflected in state and Common Core Standards, while making connections to students' authentic reading and writing experiences? The solution: mentor texts! By studying and discussing how grammatical concepts are used in published texts and the importance of those concepts to the effectiveness of the piece of writing, students can develop a deep understanding of what key grammatical concepts are and why they are important (Ruday, 2020). Through the use of mentor texts, students are able to think carefully and thoughtfully about how and why published authors use key grammatical concepts and ways they can apply those same concepts to their own writing.

An especially important benefit of mentor text-based grammar instruction is that it helps students read like writers–by examining the grammatical concepts that authors use, thinking about their importance, and ultimately considering how they can apply those concepts in their own works, students gain a deeper understanding of these concepts than if they only examined them through out-of-context worksheets (Ruday, 2020). In this approach, literature is an entryway to effective grammar instruction; it helps students understand the features and importance of the grammatical concepts they study. The idea of reading like writers is supported by the National Council of Teachers of English (NCTE), which asserts that "writing and reading are related" and recommends that teachers understand "how writers read for the purposes of writing—with an eye toward not just what the text says but how it is put together" (NCTE Professional Knowledge for the Teaching of Writing, 2016, Writing and reading are related section).

When students examine how a grammatical concept is used in a published mentor text and reflect on its significance, they can enhance their understanding of grammar by increasing their metacognition of it. Metacognition, knowledge of cognitive phenomena (Flavell, 1979), can play an important role in effective grammar instruction (Cook, 2020; Ruday, 2020) by helping students understand why a writer might have chosen to use a particular grammatical concept and what impact that concept might have on the written work. For example, let's take a look at the excerpt from Kareen Getten's (2020) book *When Life Gives You Mangos* previously featured in this chapter: "I have a secret hideout behind the house" (p. 8). By reflecting on the importance of the prepositional phrase "behind the house" and considering why the author may have chosen to include it in the work, students will develop their metacognition of the significance and impact of this concept.

When students think metacognitively about grammatical concepts, they can begin to see these concepts as tools that authors strategically use in writing and not just terms and definitions that need to be memorized. Because of this, I like to explain to students that grammatical concepts function as tools for communication that writers intentionally use in their works to maximize their effectiveness (Ruday, 2020). When I do so, I explain that, just as all tools have specific uses and are utilized purposefully based on a certain task or project, grammatical concepts also have particular uses and are best incorporated into writing with a clear understanding of how and why to use them. Like we would select a screwdriver if it is the best tool for a specific job, we would also use a prepositional phrase if it's the most effective way to add detail to a text. In the elementary school classroom, the toolkit approach can establish a foundation for students' success with grammar by helping them see at a young age how grammatical concepts can function as tools for effective writing.

The information in this section has shared key research-based findings and approaches that relate to effective grammar instruction. Based on these ideas, five especially important guidelines for teaching grammar are:

1. Teach grammar in the context of reading and writing
2. Incorporate mentor texts
3. Show students how to read like writers
4. Develop students' metacognition of grammatical concepts
5. Talk with students about how grammatical concepts are tools for effective writing.

Now, let's explore this book's approach and its connection to the best practices of grammar instruction.

This Book's Approach

The lesson plans in this book incorporate the research-based best practices of grammar instruction and apply those practices to the teaching and learning of grammar instruction in grades three, four, and five. They present grammatical concepts in the context of effective writing through the use of mentor texts. These mentor text examples, which students read from a writer's perspective, deepen students' metacognition of the importance of these concepts and help them see the elements of grammar as tools for strong writing that authors use strategically to make their work as strong as possible. The goal of the book is to provide elementary school teachers with concrete, user-friendly lesson plans that they can easily use to put mentor-text-based grammar instruction into action in their classrooms. The grammar lessons provided in this book can be woven into the instructional day in a variety of ways, depending on the needs of your students and the time you have available: each day of instruction can comprise an entire literacy block, but it can also take a portion of a given day's literacy block if you feel your students would take less time with the described activities.

These lesson plans feature published examples of grammatical concepts from contemporary children's and middle-grade books, activities that help students connect their reading and writing experiences, and reflective activities designed to facilitate students' metacognition of the importance of grammatical concepts. This book merges research and practice in concrete and direct ways: each lesson plan is based on principles of mentor text-based grammar instruction designed to deepen students' awareness of what grammatical concepts are, why they're important to effective writing, how to use them to maximize the effectiveness of their own works, and how incorporating them can enhance the quality of their own writing. The thorough plans in this book are designed to help you put the best practices of grammar instruction into action in your teaching in concrete, practitioner-oriented ways that are informed by key research findings on the teaching of grammar. The ideas, examples, and instructional suggestions will give you the necessary resources to incorporate mentor text-based grammar lessons that develop students' metacognition of the tools of effective grammar and communication.

What to Expect in This Book

This book contains 15 detailed mentor text-based lesson plans on elementary school grammar instruction, each of which will provide you with a clear and informative explanation of its focal grammatical concept, a published mentor text that exemplifies that concept, and instructional steps to use when helping your students understand the features of a grammatical concept, comprehend its importance, and connect it to their writing. For consistency and ease of use, each of the book's lesson plans follows this format:

- Overview: an overarching description of the key features and goals of the lesson.
- Objectives: an identification of key content students will learn.
- Time Frame: the number of class periods the lesson is designed to take. (While this is a recommended time frame, you should certainly feel free to adapt the time spent on the lesson to what you feel would be best for your students.)
- Background Knowledge Required: what students need to know before getting started with the lesson.
- Materials Needed: materials and resources to have on hand for the lesson.
- Detailed Plan: step-by-step directions for conducting the lesson. The detailed lesson plan provides:
  - A potential script to use with your students or adapt as needed. In each plan, the potential script is provided as a series of quotations.
  - Information about the focal concept to share with students during an introductory mini-lesson.

- One or more graphic organizers that can help students understand the grammatical concept.
- A published mentor text that exemplifies strong use of the grammatical concept.
- Ideas about how to conduct all of the lesson's instructional activities with your students.
- Additional instructional recommendations for delivering the lesson, which are included in italics.
- Differentiation Suggestions: recommendations for differentiating the lesson for students who need additional support or who have advanced understandings of the content.
- Assessment: ideas for how to assess students' understandings of the focal concept.
- Notes: a place to make notes on what worked during the lesson and what you might adapt the next time you teach it.

The 15 lesson plans in this book are divided into three sections: Lesson Plans Recommended for the Third-Grade Classroom, Lesson Plans Recommended for the Fourth-Grade Classroom, and Lesson Plans Recommended for the Fifth-Grade Classroom, with five lessons associated with each of these three grade levels. Each lesson represents a specific grammatical concept; I connected the grammatical concepts and grade levels by looking closely at a wide range of state grammar, writing, and language standards, as well as the Common Core State Language Standards, and using this information to identify grade levels at which certain grammatical concepts are often discussed. However, I encourage you not to feel limited by the grade levels associated with these grammatical concepts. My recommendation is to use all of the lesson plans in this book in the ways that best serve your students. For example, if you teach fourth grade, you might use some of the lessons from the third-grade section to ensure that your students have strong understandings of concepts that you feel are especially important, and you might also incorporate some lessons from the fifth-grade section when your students seem ready to learn that information. In addition, you could use these lessons as tools for differentiation with small groups or individual students by providing needed review and extra support with an earlier-grade lesson plan or by using an older-grade lesson plan to provide differentiated learning opportunities for students with advanced knowledge of grammar. As you put this book's lessons into action, you can sequence the lessons exactly as they are in the text, or you can make adaptations based on the needs of your students. For example, if you feel your students are ready to learn these topics in the order they are described, you can use the same scope and sequence presented in the book, but you can also teach the lessons in the order that best aligns with your students' needs. There are many ways to flexibly make use of the book's range of lesson plans in ways that best meet the needs of your students!

Figure I.1 lists all of the grammatical concepts addressed in this book and the lesson plan in which each concept is addressed.

In addition to these three sections of lesson plans, this book contains a fourth section titled "Final Thoughts and Resources." In this section, you'll first find a concluding chapter titled "Putting Mentor Text-Based Grammar Instruction Into Action in Grades Three to Five," which synthesizes key ideas from the book and shares closing suggestions for putting its lessons into practice as effectively as possible. After that, you'll encounter Appendix A: Annotated Bibliography of Mentor Texts, which is designed to provide you with a quick reference guide to all of the mentor text examples used in this book. The annotated bibliography contains the titles and authors of the works

Grammatical Concepts	Associated Lesson Plans
Subject-verb agreement	Lesson 3.1
Adjectives	Lesson 3.2
Adverbs	Lesson 3.3
Simple, compound, and complex sentences	Lesson 3.4
Using commas and quotation marks when writing dialogue	Lesson 3.5
Capitalization	Lesson 4.1
Modal auxiliaries	Lesson 4.2
Prepositional phrases	Lesson 4.3
Relative clauses	Lesson 4.4
Strong verbs and specific nouns	Lesson 4.5
Conjunctions	Lesson 5.1
Interjections	Lesson 5.2
Pronoun-antecedent agreement	Lesson 5.3
Figurative language	Lesson 5.4
Using commas for clarity	Lesson 5.5

Figure I.1 Grammatical Concepts and Associated Lesson Plans

of literature featured in this book, a key grammatical concept found in each work, and excerpt from that work, previously featured in one of the book's lesson plans, that demonstrates exactly how the author uses that grammatical concept. This annotated bibliography is also available electronically from the Routledge website so that you can have easily accessible electronic copies of these mentor texts. You'll then come to Appendix B: Reproducible Graphic Organizers. This resource contains all of the graphic organizers featured in the book's lesson plans. The graphic organizers are grouped by their corresponding lesson plans for clarity and convenient access. These graphic organizers can also be downloaded from the Routledge website to help make the book's resources as easy to use as possible. Finally, you'll find Appendix C: Lesson Plan Template. You can download this planning template and use it to follow this book's format with your own mentor texts and examples.

I believe that teaching grammar in engaging and meaningful ways that use mentor texts and develop students' metacognitive understandings of grammatical concepts is such an important way to help our students grow as writers, readers, and thinkers. By incorporating these methods in grades three, four, and five, we can help our students begin to understand the impact of grammatical concepts, facilitating their literacy success in their current work while also setting them up for continued accomplishments in the future. Now that we have explored the best practices of grammar instruction, the ways those practices align with this book's approach, and the book's key features, let's get started! Keep reading to begin your exploration of these grammar lesson plans!

References

Anderson, J. (2005). *Mechanically inclined*. Stenhouse.
Booth, C. (2014). *Kinda like brothers*. Scholastic.
Cook, L. S. (2020). Students as their own best critics: A metacognitive approach to teaching grammar in context. *ATEG Journal, 29*, 14–25.
Dorfman, L. R., & Cappelli, R. (2017). *Mentor texts: Teaching writing through children's literature, K-6* (2nd ed.). Stenhouse.
Ehmann, S., & Gayer, K. (2009). *I can write like that!: A guide to mentor texts and craft studies for writer's workshop*. International Reading Association.
Flavell, J. H. (1979). Metacognition and cognitive monitoring. *American Psychologist, 34*, 906–911.
Getten, K. (2020). *When life gives you mangos*. Yearling.
National Council of Teachers of English (2016). NCTE professional knowledge for the teaching of writing. https://ncte.org/statement/teaching-writing/

Ruday, S. (2020). *The elementary school grammar toolkit: Using mentor texts to teach standards-based language and grammar in grades 3–5*. Routledge Eye on Education.

Smagorinsky, P. (2018). *Teaching English by design: How to create and carry out instructional units*. Heinemann.

Weaver, (1998). Teaching grammar in the context of writing. In C. Weaver (Ed.), *Lessons to share on teaching grammar in context* (pp. 18–38). Boynton/Cook.

Wotjer, S. (1998). Facilitating the use of description—and grammar. In C. Weaver (Ed.), *Lessons to share on teaching grammar in context* (pp. 95–99). Boynton/Cook.

SECTION ONE

Lesson Plans Recommended for the Third-Grade Classroom

LESSON 3.1

Let's Agree

Subject-Verb Agreement

Overview

This lesson focuses on the concept of subject-verb agreement, which is the idea that subjects and verbs must match in number: singular subjects go with singular verbs, and plural subjects go with plural verbs. The lesson spans two class periods. On day one, students will learn the features of subject-verb agreement, see examples of it, examine how it appears in published texts, and consider its impact on writing. On day two, students will review this concept, apply it to their own writing, and reflect on how subject-verb agreement is important to the effectiveness of their works. At the conclusion of the instructional process, students will consider how this concept can be important to their future writing.

Objectives

- Students will understand the concept of subject-verb agreement, including the reasons subject-verb agreement is present in specific examples.
- Students will understand the importance of subject-verb agreement to strong writing.
- Students will be able to apply the concept of subject-verb agreement to their writing and reflect on the importance of doing so.

DOI: 10.4324/9781003610656-3

Time Frame

Two class periods.

Background Knowledge Required

Students will need background knowledge of subjects and verbs. Students should also understand the forms of the verb "be."

Materials Needed

- Figures 3.1.1–3.1.6. These figures are available in the lesson plan, in Appendix B: Reproducible Graphic Organizers, and in electronic format on the book's website.
- A board, projector, or piece of chart paper for displaying information.
- Paper for students' writing activities.

Detailed Plan

Day One
1. Introduction
To begin this instructional process, you'll introduce students to the topic of subject-verb agreement, share the key questions they'll investigate on their first day working on this topic, and present the day's agenda.

"Today, we're going to explore an important grammatical concept: subject-verb agreement. We'll examine these questions:

- What is subject-verb agreement?
- What are some ways that subject-verb agreement can look?
- Why is subject-verb agreement important to strong writing?

Here is the agenda for our work today:

- Subject-verb agreement mini-lesson
- Mentor text examples
- Mentor text discussion and analysis activities
- Exit question"

I recommend displaying the day's questions and agenda items while sharing them with students.

2. Subject-Verb Agreement Mini-Lesson

You'll now conduct a mini-lesson on the concept of subject-verb agreement. In this lesson, you'll introduce students to what subject-verb agreement is, discuss key ideas related to it, provide examples of it, and describe its importance.

"In this mini-lesson, I'll share some important information about subject-verb agreement. This is the first step in our work together on this topic. Let's start with what subject-verb agreement is. Subject-verb agreement is the idea that subjects and verbs must match in number: singular subjects go with singular verbs, and plural subjects go with plural verbs. So, if the subject of a sentence I'm writing is 'five dogs,' which is plural, I would need for my verb to also match the plural form. My sentence could be 'Five dogs jump in the air.' In this sentence, the verb 'jump' aligns with the plural subject of 'five dogs.' If my subject was 'one dog,' my sentence could read 'One dog jumps in the air.' Here, the verb 'jumps' goes with the singular subject of 'one dog.' Let's look together at a chart that contains key ideas about subject-verb agreement."

Grammatical Concept	What Is Subject-Verb Agreement?	What Are Some Key Ideas to Know About Subject-Verb Agreement?	Why Is Subject-Verb Agreement Important to Strong Writing?
Subject-verb agreement	Subject-verb agreement is the idea that subjects and verbs must match in number: singular subjects go with singular verbs, and plural subjects go with plural verbs.	Not all verbs change based on whether the subject is singular or plural. For example, in the sentence "The goats walked," the verb would be "walked" whether the subject is singular or plural. A situation in which a verb changes based on whether the subject is singular or plural is in third-person narration in the present tense. For instance, the sentence "The goat walks" becomes "The goats walk" if the subject goes from singular to plural.	Subject-verb agreement is important to strong writing because it helps readers clearly understand what the writer is expressing. If there is confusion in subject-verb agreement, readers could be distracted or not correctly understand a statement.

Figure 3.1.1 Subject-Verb Agreement Information

(Continued)

Grammatical Concept	What Is Subject-Verb Agreement?	What Are Some Key Ideas to Know About Subject-Verb Agreement?	Why Is Subject-Verb Agreement Important to Strong Writing?
		The verb also frequently changes based on whether a subject is singular or plural when that verb is a form of "be." For example, the sentence "The goat was outside" uses the singular verb "was" to go with its singular subject. "The goats were outside" uses the plural verb "were" to go with its plural subject.	

Figure 3.1.1 (Continued)

I recommend displaying this chart on a projector screen while discussing its information with students.

3. Mentor Text Examples

Here, you'll share with students published examples of sentences that contain subject-verb agreement. The mentor text examples featured here represent the three types of subject-verb agreement referred to in Figure 3.1.1: a sentence in which the verb does not change based on whether the subject is singular or plural, a sentence with third-person narration in the present tense, and a sentence containing a form of the verb "be." These examples show students how subject-verb agreement is used authentically in writing.

"We'll now look at published examples of subject-verb agreement. I'm going to show you three subject-verb agreement mentor texts from published books. One is a sentence in which the verb does not change based on whether the subject is singular or plural, the next one is a sentence with third-person narration in the present tense, and the final one is a sentence containing a form of the verb 'be.' Let's check out these sentences."

Example One: Verb Does Not Change Based on Whether Subject Is Singular or Plural	Example Two: Third-Person Narration in Present Tense	Example Three: Sentence Containing Form of the Verb "Be"
"At the top of the cliff, Zoe sniffed the air" (Gibbs, 2023, p. 5).	"She speaks slowly and politely" (Elliott, 2019, p. 2).	"He was so excited!" (Reed, 2021, p. 5).

Figure 3.1.2 Subject-Verb Agreement Mentor Text Examples

I suggest displaying these mentor text examples on a slide or piece of chart paper and reading them aloud while students follow along.

4. Mentor Text Discussion and Analysis Activities

At this point in the instructional process, you'll support students as they discuss and analyze the subject-verb agreement in the mentor text examples. This work is designed to develop students' understandings of the importance of subject-verb agreement.

"Now that we've seen published examples of subject-verb agreement, we'll think about the importance of subject-verb agreement to those examples. We'll look at each published example compared with a revised version that does not contain subject-verb agreement. Then, we'll discuss why the subject-verb agreement in the original sentence is important to its effectiveness.

Let's get started with our first mentor text example. In this example, the verb in the original passage doesn't change based on whether the subject is singular or plural. The revised version uses a different verb tense and incorrect subject-verb agreement."

Original Mentor Text Example	Revised Example That Does Not Contain Subject-Verb Agreement	Why the Subject-Verb Agreement Is Important to the Original Example
"At the top of the cliff, Zoe sniffed the air" (Gibbs, 2023, p. 5).	At the top of the cliff, Zoe and I sniffs the air.	

Figure 3.1.3 Subject-Verb Agreement Discussion Example One: Original Verb Does Not Change Based on Whether Subject Is Singular or Plural

I recommend displaying this chart, reading both examples aloud, talking with students about why they think the subject-verb agreement is important in the original to their ability to understand what is taking place in that sentence, and writing highlights of their response in the right-hand column. During this discussion, you can encourage students to compare the clarity of the original example with the revised one and talk with them about why the revised sentence is harder to understand.

"Let's now discuss our second mentor text example, which uses third-person narration in the present tense. We'll see the original example and a revised version that doesn't contain subject-verb agreement."

Original Mentor Text Example	Revised Example That Does Not Contain Subject-Verb Agreement	Why the Subject-Verb Agreement Is Important to the Original Example
"She speaks slowly and politely" (Elliott, 2019, p. 2).	She speak slowly and politely.	

Figure 3.1.4 Subject-Verb Agreement Discussion Example Two: Third Person Narration in Present Tense

I suggest displaying this chart, reading the examples out loud, and asking students why they think the subject-verb agreement in the original sentence is important to its clarity and effectiveness. Students can consider how the subject-verb agreement in the first sentence helps readers understand that there is a singular subject that goes with its singular verb. I recommend writing highlights from students' responses in the right-hand column.

"We'll now analyze our third example, which contains a form of the verb 'be,' by looking at the original sentence and a revised version without subject-verb agreement."

Original Mentor Text Example	Revised Example That Does Not Contain Subject-Verb Agreement	Why the Subject-Verb Agreement Is Important to the Original Example
"He was so excited!" (Reed, 2021, p. 5).	He and his friend was so excited!	

Figure 3.1.5 Subject-Verb Agreement Discussion Example Three: Sentence Containing Form of the Verb "Be"

You can display this chart, read aloud its examples, ask students to consider the importance of the subject-verb agreement to the original text, and record response highlights in the third column. Students can reflect on how the subject-verb agreement in the original sentence makes it clear to readers that there is only one subject being described.

5. Exit Question

This session concludes with an exit question on the importance of subject-verb agreement to strong writing.

"To close our work for today on subject-verb agreement, you'll answer an exit question about this concept by writing your answer on a piece of paper. I'll then ask for two volunteers to share, and I'll collect everyone's work. The exit question is 'Why is subject-verb agreement important to strong writing?'"

I recommend displaying the question while you read it and students write their answers. After collecting students' responses, I suggest examining them to evaluate how well students understand the topic and using that information to inform your upcoming instruction.

Day Two
1. Introduction

You'll begin the second day of work on subject-verb agreement by discussing how the day's work builds on the previous day's lesson, sharing the day's focal questions, and presenting the agenda.

"Wonderful work yesterday on subject-verb agreement! Yesterday, we discussed what subject-verb agreement is, explored some forms it can take, examined and analyzed published examples of it, and answered an exit question about its importance to strong writing. Today, we'll build on that work and explore subject-verb agreement in more depth. First, we'll review key information about subject-verb agreement. Next, we'll create our own examples of subject-verb agreement and reflect on what we wrote. We'll finish with an exit question about the importance of subject-verb agreement to our future writing. Today's key questions are:

- How can we use subject-verb agreement in our writing?
- How is subject-verb agreement important to the quality of our writing?

Here is today's agenda:

- Subject-verb agreement review
- Writing activity
- Reflection
- Exit question"

I suggest displaying the key questions and agenda items while reading them aloud.

2. Subject-Verb Agreement Review

Next, you'll review important information, ideas, and examples from the previous day's work on subject-verb agreement.

"We'll review important information about subject-verb agreement we discussed yesterday. Let's look at a chart that reviews what subject-verb agreement is, key ideas to know about it, why it's important to strong writing, and published examples of it."

What Is Subject-Verb Agreement?	What Are Some Key Ideas to Know About Subject-Verb Agreement?	Why Is Subject-Verb Agreement Important to Strong Writing?	What Are Published Examples of Subject-Verb Agreement?
Subject-verb agreement is the idea that subjects and verbs must match in number: singular subjects go with singular verbs, and plural subjects go with plural verbs.	Not all verbs change based on whether the subject is singular or plural. For example, in the sentence "The goats walked," the verb would be "walked" whether the subject is singular or plural. A situation in which a verb changes based on whether the subject is singular or plural is in third-person narration in the present tense. For instance, the sentence "The goat walks" becomes "The goats walk" if the subject goes from singular to plural.	Subject-verb agreement is important to strong writing because it helps readers clearly understand what the writer is expressing. If there is confusion in subject-verb agreement, readers could be distracted or not correctly understand a statement.	Example One: Verb Does Not Change Based on Whether Subject Is Singular or Plural: "At the top of the cliff, Zoe sniffed the air" (Gibbs, 2023, p. 5). Third-Person Narration in Present Tense: "She speaks slowly and politely" (Elliott, 2019, p. 2). Sentence Containing Form of the Verb "Be": "He was so excited!" (Reed, 2021, p. 5).

Figure 3.1.6 Subject-Verb Agreement Review Information

(Continued)

What Is Subject-Verb Agreement?	What Are Some Key Ideas to Know About Subject-Verb Agreement?	Why Is Subject-Verb Agreement Important to Strong Writing?	What Are Published Examples of Subject-Verb Agreement?
	The verb also frequently changes based on whether a subject is singular or plural when that verb is a form of "be." For example, the sentence "The goat was outside" uses the singular verb "was" to go with its singular subject. "The goats were outside" uses the plural verb "were" to go with its plural subject.		

Figure 3.1.6 (Continued)

I suggest displaying this chart and reading its contents aloud while students follow along. If students have shown confusion about any information regarding subject-verb agreement, this is a great time to discuss that information.

3. Writing Activity

In this writing activity, students create their own examples of subject-verb agreement and identify why subject-verb agreement is present in that example.

"We'll apply what we've learned about subject-verb agreement to our own writing! You'll create a sentence that contains subject-verb agreement and explain why subject-verb agreement is present in that sentence."

"First, I'll share with you an example I wrote: 'The bird flies in the air.' This sentence contains subject-verb agreement because it is written in third-person narration in the present tense and uses a singular subject—'bird'—and a singular verb—'flies.'"

When you teach this lesson, you can use this same example or create your own to share with students.

"Now, it's time for you to create your own example of subject-verb agreement and write an explanation of why the sentence you created contains subject-verb agreement. After you do this, I'll ask volunteers to share with the class."

As students write, I recommend circulating the classroom, checking in on their work, and providing praise and *support.*

"Great job, everyone! We'll take two volunteers to share with the rest of us the sentence they created and why that sentence contains subject-verb agreement."

After students share their work, I suggest identifying strong work while also providing any needed clarification.

4. Reflection

Next, students revisit the work they did in the writing activity and reflect on why the subject-verb agreement in the sentence they wrote is important to the effectiveness of that sentence.

"In this next activity, you'll reflect on the importance of subject-verb agreement to the sentence you wrote. You'll write an answer to this question: 'Why is the subject-verb agreement in the sentence you wrote important to the effectiveness of the sentence?'"

I recommend posting this question while reading it aloud.

"I'll share the reflection I wrote about my sentence, 'The bird flies in the air.' I said, 'The subject-verb agreement between the subject bird and the verb flies is important because it helps readers understand what I am expressing. It shows that there is one bird in the sentence. If the subject-verb agreement was confusing, readers could be unsure how many birds I'm describing.'"

If you use this example, you can share this reflection with your students. If you write your own passage, you can share a reflection that aligns with that passage.

"Now, you'll revisit the sentence you created and write a response to the question 'Why is the subject-verb agreement in the sentence you wrote important to the effectiveness of the sentence?'"

As students reflect, I suggest moving around the classroom to check on their progress and provide support.

"Great job. Let's have two volunteers share their reflection question responses out loud. Then, everyone will turn in their reflections and the sentences you wrote during the writing activity."

5. Exit Question

This sequence closes with students answering an exit question about the importance of subject-verb agreement to their future writing.

"To finish our work on subject-verb agreement, you'll answer an exit question. After you write your answer, volunteers will share. I'll then collect everyone's responses. The exit question is 'How can subject-verb agreement be important to your future writing?'"

I suggest displaying this question and reading it aloud. When students share their answers, I compliment strong statements and provide elaboration and clarification when relevant.

Differentiation Suggestions

There are many differentiation options for this lesson:

- Students can explore additional subject-verb agreement mentor texts to give them increased exposure to how this concept can look in published writing.
- Students can examine mentor texts on a range of reading levels so they can work with texts that fit them well.
- Students can create multiple examples of subject-verb agreement in the writing activity.
- Students can create examples that represent different forms of subject-verb agreement.

Assessment

I suggest assessing students' knowledge of subject-verb agreement and their work in this lesson sequence in two ways:

- Students' exit question responses.
  - The two exit question responses students write during this instructional process provide key insight into their knowledge of subject-verb agreement and its importance to strong writing. When assessing students' responses to the day-one exit question, "Why is subject-verb agreement important to strong writing?," I recommend evaluating how well students explain that subject-verb agreement is important because it helps readers understand what the writer is expressing. When evaluating students' work on the day-two exit question, "How can subject-verb agreement be important to your future writing?," I suggest assessing how well students explain that they can use subject-verb agreement in their future work to help their readers understand what they are communicating.

- Students' written examples and reflections.
  - I recommend assessing students' understandings of subject-verb agreement and its importance by reading their work from the writing activity and their corresponding reflections. When assessing students' work from the writing activity, I look to see if their sentences contain subject-verb agreement and if they accurately explained why subject-verb is present in those sentences. When evaluating students' reflections, I assess the detail and insight they used when discussing why subject-verb agreement is important to the sentences they created.

Notes

- What worked when teaching this lesson?

- What might you adapt or change the next time you teach it?

References

Elliott, Z. (2019). *Dragons in a bag*. Yearling.
Gibbs, S. (2023). *Spy school goes north*. Simon & Schuster Books for Young Readers.
Reed, D. (2021). *Simon B. Rhymin*. Little, Brown and Company.

LESSON 3.2

Descriptive Information

Adjectives

Overview

This lesson focuses on the grammatical concept of adjectives, which are descriptive words that provide information about a noun or pronoun. The lesson spans two class periods. On the first day, students will learn about the features of adjectives, see examples of them, explore how writers use them, and consider their impact on writing. On the second day, students will review key information about adjectives, apply them to their own writing, and reflect on the significance of those adjectives. To conclude the process, students will answer an exit question about the importance of adjectives to strong writing.

Objectives

- Students will understand the concept of adjectives.
- Students will understand the importance of adjectives to strong writing.
- Students will be able to use adjectives in their writing and reflect on the importance of doing so.

Time Frame

Two class periods.

DOI: 10.4324/9781003610656-4

Background Knowledge Required

Students will need knowledge of nouns and pronouns to understand what adjectives describe.

Materials Needed

- Figures 3.2.1–3.2.4. These figures are available in the lesson plan, in Appendix B: Reproducible Graphic Organizers, and in electronic format on the book's website.
- A board, projector, or piece of chart paper for displaying information.
- Paper for students' writing activities.

Detailed Plan

Day One
1. Introduction

To introduce this instructional process, you'll first let students know that they'll be studying adjectives. Then, you'll present the key questions about adjectives the class will explore that day. After that, you'll share the day's agenda.

"We're going to learn about the grammatical concept of adjectives. Adjectives are descriptive words that provide information about a noun or pronoun. We'll think about these questions today:

- What are adjectives?
- Why are adjectives important to strong writing?

Now, let's check out today's agenda. It lists the activities we'll do as we learn about adjectives:

- Adjective mini-lesson
- Mentor text example
- Mentor text discussion and analysis activities
- Exit question"

I suggest displaying the day's questions and agenda items while sharing them with students.

2. Adjective Mini-Lesson

Here, you'll teach a mini-lesson on key features of adjectives. In it, you'll introduce students to what adjectives are, provide examples of adjectives, and discuss the importance of this concept.

"In this mini-lesson, I'll share some important information about adjectives. This is the starting point for the work we'll do together on adjectives. We'll continue to discuss these ideas in more detail as we continue to learn about adjectives.

First, let's talk about what adjectives are. Adjectives are descriptive words that provide information about a noun or pronoun. For example, in the sentence 'They looked at a colorful picture,' the word 'colorful' is an adjective. It provides descriptive information about the picture. Similarly, in the sentence, 'We saw a cute cat,' 'cute' is an adjective. This word describes the cat. Another example is in the sentence, 'Sam played a fun game.' 'Fun' is an adjective that describes the game. All of these words provide descriptive information that helps the reader understand the features of the noun being described. Since adjectives can boost the reader's knowledge of the noun or pronoun they're describing, they're important tools for strong writing. I'm going to share with you an informational chart on adjectives. It contains key information about what adjectives are, what they look like, how they're used, and why they're important to strong writing."

Grammatical Concept	What Are Adjectives?	What Are Some Examples of Adjectives?	What Are Some Ways Adjectives Can Look in Writing?	Why Are Adjectives Important to Strong Writing?
Adjectives	Adjectives are descriptive words that provide information about a noun or pronoun.	Some examples of adjectives are colorful, cute, fun, young, old, hot, cold, beautiful, special, large, small, fast, and happy.	The **happy** fans cheered. We felt the **cold** wind. We saw a **large** elephant at the zoo.	Adjectives are important to strong writing because they help the reader understand the features of the noun or pronoun being described.

Figure 3.2.1 Adjective Information

I suggest projecting this chart on a screen or recreating it on chart paper while talking with students about this information.

3. Mentor Text Example

At this point in the lesson, you'll share with students a published passage in which an author uses adjectives to provide descriptive information. By doing so, you'll show students how adjectives are used authentically and prepare them for other work they'll do later in this lesson.

"Let's now deepen our knowledge of adjectives by looking at a published example. We'll look together at an adjective example from the book *The Creature of the Pines* by Adam Gidwitz: 'Elliot Eisner stood at the front of the bus, looking down the long aisle' (Gidwitz, 2018, p. 1). In this passage, author Adam Gidwitz uses the adjective 'long' to add descriptive information. In our next activity, we'll explore the importance of this adjective to the passage."

When you share this adjective mentor text example with students, I recommend displaying it on a slide or piece of chart paper so that students can read along with you.

4. Mentor Text Discussion and Analysis Activities

In this stage of the lesson, you'll lead students through a discussion about the adjective mentor text and through related activities designed to help them understand the importance of the adjective to the text. The goal of this work is to facilitate students' awareness of the role of adjectives in writing.

"We're going to think together about why the adjective 'long' is important to the mentor text example from *The Creature of the Pines* that we examined. Let's compare the original text with a revised version that doesn't contain the adjective."

Original Text	Revised Version With Adjective Removed
"Elliot Eisner stood at the front of the bus, looking down the long aisle" (Gidwitz, 2018, p. 1).	Elliot Eisner stood at the front of the bus, looking down the aisle.

Figure 3.2.2 Original Text vs. Revised Version with Adjective Removed

I suggest projecting these examples to the front of the classroom or recreating them on chart paper so that students can follow along.

"For our next step, please talk with a partner about these two questions: How is the sentence different without the adjective 'long'? and Why do you think the author used this adjective in the sentence? After you talk with your partners, I'll ask for volunteers to share with the class. We'll record responses on a graphic organizer that I'll display."

Reflection Question One	**Reflection Question Two**
How is the sentence different without the adjective "long"?	Why do you think the author used this adjective in the sentence?

Figure 3.2.3 Adjective Reflection Questions Graphic Organizer

I recommend projecting this chart or recreating it on chart paper and then recording students' responses on the chart when they share their ideas.

5. Exit Question

At the conclusion of this class period, students answer an exit question regarding the importance of adjectives.

"To finish our work on adjectives for today, you'll answer an exit question on this topic. Please write your response on a piece of paper. After you write, I'll ask for two volunteers to share, and I'll collect everyone's answers. The exit question is 'Why would writers use adjectives in their work?'"

I suggest displaying this question as you read it and while students write their answers. When students submit their responses, I examine the answers to evaluate their understanding. I use this information to inform my upcoming instruction on the topic.

Day Two
1. Introduction
To begin the second day of work on adjectives, you'll discuss how the work students will do that day builds on the previous day's lesson, provide the day's focal questions, and share the class period's agenda.

"Great job yesterday working on adjectives! In yesterday's class, we discussed what adjectives are and why they're important. After that, we looked at a published example of adjective use from the book *The Creature of the Pines* (Gidwitz, 2018). We then reflected on the impact of the adjective in that passage before closing with an exit question about why writers use adjectives. Today, we'll build on that work and go into even more depth with adjectives. First, we'll review important information about adjectives. Then, we'll use adjectives in our own writing and think about their significance. Afterwards, we'll consider why adjectives are important tools for strong writing. Here are our key questions for today:

- How can we use adjectives in our writing?
- How can adjectives impact the description and detail in our writing?

Here is our agenda for today:

- Adjective review
- Writing activity
- Reflection
- Exit question"

I like to display the key questions and agenda items while sharing them with students.

2. Adjective Review
Here, you'll review key ideas, examples, and explanations about adjectives you shared and discussed in the previous day's work.

"Let's review some key information about adjectives that we discussed yesterday. We'll look together at a chart that reviews what adjectives are, shares examples of them, explains why they're important to strong writing, and provides a published example of their use."

What Are Adjectives?	What Are Some Examples of Adjectives?	Why Are Adjectives Important to Strong Writing?	What Is a Published Example of Adjective Use?
Adjectives are descriptive words that provide information about a noun or pronoun.	Some examples of adjectives are colorful, cute, fun, young, old, hot, cold, beautiful, special, large, small, fast, and happy.	Adjectives are important to strong writing because they help the reader understand the features of the noun or pronoun being described.	"Elliot Eisner stood at the front of the bus, looking down the **long** aisle" (Gidwitz, 2018, p. 1).

Figure 3.2.4 Adjective Review Information

I recommend displaying this chart and reading the information on it out loud while students follow along. This is also a great time to discuss any adjective information that may have been confusing to students in the previous day's class.

3. Writing Activity

In this activity, students apply adjectives to their writing. They create a brief passage that uses an adjective to provide descriptive information about a noun or pronoun.

"We're going to take what we've learned about adjectives and put it into action in our own writing! You'll create a one- or two-sentence passage that uses an adjective to describe a noun or pronoun. You can write about the topic of your choice—the only requirement is to use an adjective in your work!

Before you start, I'll share an example I created: 'We sat by the warm fireplace.' In this sentence, I used the adjective 'warm' to provide descriptive information. I underlined the adjective I used."

When teaching this lesson, you can use this adjective example or create your own to share with your students.

"It's your turn! You'll create a passage that uses an adjective to provide description, and you'll underline the adjective in your passage like I did in the example. Afterwards, I'll ask you to share your work with a partner. Volunteers will share with the class."

While students work on these examples, I suggest moving around the classroom and monitoring their progress. This is a great time to provide support and praise strong work.

"Good job working on those examples. Next, share with a partner the passage you created and identify the adjective you used."

During this time, I recommend circulating and listening to what students share. This is another excellent opportunity to support students and praise excellent work.

"Let's have two volunteers share with the class the passage you created, identifying the adjective you used in it."

While students share these ideas with the class, I like to praise strong work and provide relevant explanations and information.

4. Reflection

Students now return to the passage they created in the previous writing activity and analyze the importance of the adjective they used in the piece they wrote.

"In our next activity, you'll think about the importance of the adjective that you used in the passage you just wrote. You'll write an answer to the question 'Why is the adjective you used in your passage important?'"

I suggest posting this question while sharing it with students.

"Before you do this, I'll share the reflection I wrote about my passage, 'We sat by the warm fireplace.' My answer to the reflection question is 'The adjective warm is important because of the description it provides. By using this adjective, I give readers descriptive information about the fireplace and let them know that it was warm. Without the adjective, readers wouldn't have this description.'"

If you choose to use this same example with your students, you can share this reflection with them. If you create your own passage, you can model your own reflection based on that passage.

"It's your turn now. Revisit the passage you created that uses an adjective and write an answer to the question 'Why is the adjective you used in your passage important?'"

While students compose these responses, I recommend circulating the classroom to monitor their progress and providing them with individualized feedback.

"Good work writing those responses. Please share with a partner the reflection you created and listen as they share theirs."

As students share with partners, I like listening to their insights and commenting on their ideas.

"Let's take two volunteers to share their answers to the reflection question with the class. After that, I'll ask for all of you to turn in these reflections and the passages you created during the writing activity."

When students share their answers, I suggest calling attention to particularly strong reflections and building on any statements that can be further developed.

5. Exit Question

This instructional process closes with students responding to an exit question on the importance of adjectives.

"We'll conclude this work with an exit question on adjectives. You'll write an answer to an exit question on adjectives, and then I'll ask for volunteers to share their responses. After that, I'll collect all of the written answers. The exit question is 'Why are adjectives important tools for strong writing?'"

I suggest displaying the exit question while reading it. When students share their responses, I like to commend especially strong insights and comment further on statements that can benefit from additional explanation.

Differentiation Suggestions

This lesson can be differentiated in a number of ways:

- Students can work with additional adjective mentor texts so they encounter additional examples of adjectives in published writing.
- Students can work with published examples on differing reading levels so they can read texts that best fit them.
- Students can use multiple adjectives in the passages they create.
- Students can create multiple passages that use adjectives.

Assessment

I recommend assessing students' knowledge of adjectives and their work in this instructional sequence in two ways:

- Students' exit question responses.
  - The two exit question responses students compose during this instructional process provide important information about their understanding of adjectives and the role of this concept in strong writing. When evaluating students' responses to the day-one exit question, "Why would writers use adjectives in their work?," I suggest assessing how well students explain that writers would use adjectives to add descriptive information to their writing. When examining students' answers to the day-two exit question, "Why are adjectives important tools for strong writing?," I recommend assessing if students are able to explain that adjectives are important because the information in them

helps the reader understand the features of the noun or pronoun they are describing.
- Students' writing activities and corresponding reflections.
    - I suggest also assessing students' knowledge of adjectives and their importance by reading students' work from the writing activity and corresponding reflection they did on the second day of the instructional process. To assess students' work from the writing activity, I look to see if students used an adjective in their passage, if this adjective adds descriptive information, and if the descriptive information it provides aligns with the passage. When evaluating students' reflections, I assess the detail and insight in their statements about the importance of the adjective they used.

Notes

- What worked when teaching this lesson?

- What might you adapt or change the next time you teach it?

Reference

Gidwitz, A. (2018). *The creature of the pines*. Dutton Children's Books.

LESSON 3.3

The Power of Explanation

Adverbs

Overview

This lesson focuses on adverbs, which are words that describe verbs, adjectives, and other adverbs. They answer questions like "How?," "When?," "Where?," and "To what extent?" The lesson spans two class periods. On day one, students will learn key information about adverbs, examine examples of them, see how writers use them, and reflect on their importance to writing. On day two, students will review important ideas about adverbs, use them in their own writing, and consider the importance of the adverbs they used. The process concludes with students answering an exit question about the importance of adverbs to strong writing.

Objectives

- Students will understand the concept of adverbs.
- Students will understand the importance of adverbs to strong writing.
- Students will be able to use adverbs in their writing and reflect on the importance of doing so.

Time Frame

Two class periods.

DOI: 10.4324/9781003610656-5

Background Knowledge Required

Students will need to understand what verbs and adjectives are when learning about the kinds of words adverbs can describe.

Materials Needed

- Figures 3.3.1–3.3.4, which are available in the lesson plan, in Appendix B: Reproducible Graphic Organizers, and in electronic format on the book's website.
- A board, projector, or piece of chart paper to display information.
- Paper for students' writing.

Detailed Plan

Day One
1. Introduction

When introducing this instructional process, you'll first inform students that they'll be studying adverbs. Next, you'll share the key question about adverbs the class will consider that day. Then, you'll go over the agenda for the class period.

"We're going to explore the grammatical concept of adverbs. Adverbs are words that describe verbs, adjectives, and other adverbs. They provide explanations and answer questions like 'How?,' 'When?,' 'Where?,' and 'To what extent?' We'll examine these questions today:

- What are adverbs?
- Why are adverbs important to strong writing?

Today's agenda is:

- Adverb mini-lesson
- Mentor text example
- Mentor text discussion and analysis activities
- Exit question"

I recommend displaying the focal questions and agenda items while reading them aloud.

2. Adverb Mini-Lesson

Now, you'll teach a mini-lesson on key aspects of adverbs. In the lesson, you'll introduce students to what adverbs are, provide examples, and share ideas about the importance of adverbs to strong writing.

"In this mini-lesson, I'll share key information about adverbs. These ideas will be the foundation for the work we'll do on this topic. We'll discuss this information in more detail as we continue to study adverbs."

"We'll begin with what adverbs are. Adverbs are words that describe verbs, adjectives, and other adverbs. They answer questions like 'How?,' 'When?,' 'Where?,' and 'To what extent?' Many adverbs end with the letters 'ly,' but there are also many adverbs that don't end that way. We'll look at an example of adverb use. In the sentence 'The manatee swam slowly,' 'slowly' is an adverb. It describes how the manatee swam and explains what is happening in the sentence. Adverbs are important tools for strong writing because the explanation they give can help readers understand what the author is communicating. I'll share a chart that contains key information about adverbs. It contains information about what adverbs are, identifies examples of them, shows some ways they can look in writing, and discusses their importance to strong writing."

Grammatical Concept	What Are Adverbs?	What Are Some Examples of Adverbs?	What Are Some Ways Adverbs Can Look in Writing?	Why Are Adverbs Important to Strong Writing?
Adverbs	Adverbs are words that describe verbs, adjectives, and other adverbs. They answer questions like "How?," "When?," "Where?," and "To What Extent?"	Some examples of words that can function as adverbs are quickly, slowly, carefully, wildly, extremely, soon, often, frequently, immediately, happily, everywhere, exactly, truly, and very.	The fans **quickly** went to their seats. We walked **carefully** through the woods. I **immediately** recognized you. I searched **everywhere**. We'll see them **soon**. She ran **very** fast.	Adverbs are important to strong writing because the explanation they give can help readers understand what the author is communicating.

Figure 3.3.1 Adverb Information

I suggest displaying this chart or recreating it on chart paper while sharing its information with students.

3. Mentor Text Example

Next, you'll share with students a published passage in which the author uses an adverb to provide explanation. This shows students an authentic example of adverb use and prepares them for upcoming work in this instructional process.

"We'll now look at a published example of adverb use. In the book *The Scroll of Chaos*, author Elsie Chapman (2023) uses the adverb 'clumsily' in the sentence 'As Libby Pearson (my best friend) puts away her violin beside me, she clumsily bangs the instrument against the leg of her chair' (p. 1). Chapman's use of this adverb adds explanation to the sentence. Next, we'll think further about the importance of this adverb to the text."

I recommend displaying the mentor text example on a slide or piece of chart paper when sharing it with students.

4. Mentor Text Discussion and Analysis Activities

At this point in the lesson, you'll discuss the adverb mentor text with students and lead them through activities designed to help them consider the significance of the adverb "clumsily" in the sentence. The goal of this work is to develop students' understandings of the importance of adverbs in writing.

"We'll work together to consider why the adverb 'clumsily' is important to the mentor text example from *The Scroll of Chaos*. First, we'll compare the original text with a revised version that does not contain that adverb."

Original Text	**Revised Version With Adverb Removed**
"As Libby Pearson (my best friend) puts away her violin beside me, she clumsily bangs the instrument against the leg of her chair" (Chapman, 2023, p. 1).	As Libby Pearson (my best friend) puts away her violin beside me, she bangs the instrument against the leg of her chair.

Figure 3.3.2 Original Text vs. Revised Version with Adverb Removed

I suggest displaying this chart on a slide or a piece of chart paper to make it easily visible for students.

"Next, please talk with a partner about these questions: How is the sentence different without the adverb 'clumsily'? and Why do you think the author used this adverb in the sentence? After you and your partner talk, volunteers will share with the class. We'll record responses on a graphic organizer."

Reflection Question One	Reflection Question Two
How is the sentence different without the adverb "clumsily"?	Why do you think the author used this adverb in the sentence?

Figure 3.3.3 Adverb Reflection Questions Graphic Organizer

I recommend projecting this chart or recreating it on chart paper and recording students' responses on it.

5. Exit Question

To conclude this class period, students answer an exit question on the importance of adverbs.

"We'll wrap up our work on adverbs for today with an exit question. You'll write your answer to the exit question on a piece of paper. Afterward, I'll ask for two volunteers to share their ideas, and I'll collect everyone's work. The exit question is 'Why would writers use adverbs in their writing?'"

I like to display the exit question while I read it and students write their responses. After students turn in their answers, I review that information to evaluate students' understanding and inform my future instruction.

Day Two
1. Introduction

You'll begin the second day of work on adverbs by explaining how what the students will do that day builds on the previous day's work, sharing the day's key questions, and providing the agenda for the class period.

"Excellent work on adverbs yesterday! In yesterday's class, you learned key information about adverbs, examined an adverb mentor text from the book *The Scroll of Chaos* by Elsie Chapman (2023), thought about the importance of the adverb 'clumsily' to that mentor text, and answered an exit question about why writers would use adverbs in their work. In today's class, we'll build on yesterday's work and explore adverbs even more. We'll start by reviewing important adverb information. Then, we'll use adverbs in our own writing and think about their significance. After that, we'll think about why adverbs are important tools for strong writing. Our key questions for today are:

- How can we use adverbs in our writing?
- How can adverbs provide explanation in our writing?

Here is today's agenda:

- Adverb review
- Writing activity
- Reflection
- Exit question"

I suggest displaying the key questions and agenda items while sharing them with students.

2. Adverb Review

In this section of the lesson, you'll review key adverb-related information, examples, and ideas discussed the preceding day.

"Let's review important ideas about adverbs that we talked about yesterday. We'll examine a chart that reviews what adverbs are, provides examples of them, discusses their importance, and identifies a published example."

What Are Adverbs?	What Are Some Examples of Adverbs?	Why Are Adverbs Important to Strong Writing?	What Is a Published Example of Adverb Use?
Adverbs are words that describe verbs, adjectives, and other adverbs. They answer questions like "How?," "When?," "Where?," and "To What Extent?"	Some examples of words that can function as adverbs are quickly, slowly, carefully, wildly, extremely, soon, often, frequently, immediately, happily, everywhere, exactly, truly, and very.	Adverbs are important to strong writing because the explanation they give can help readers understand what the author is communicating.	"As Libby Pearson (my best friend) puts away her violin beside me, she **clumsily** bangs the instrument against the leg of her chair" (Chapman, 2023, p. 1).

Figure 3.3.4 Adverb Review Information

I like displaying this chart and reading its information aloud while students follow along. If students expressed any confusion or misunderstanding about adverbs in the previous class, I use this opportunity to provide any needed clarification.

3. Writing Activity

This writing activity asks students to apply the concept of adverbs to their writing. They create a brief passage that uses an adverb to provide explanation.

"Now, we'll take another step in our adverb work by using adverbs in our writing! You'll write a one- or two-sentence passage that uses an adverb to provide explanation to that passage. You can choose your topic—the only requirement is to use an adverb in your passage."

"Before you write, I'll share an example I created of a passage that uses an adverb: 'She proudly accepted the trophy.' I used the adverb 'proudly' to explain how the character accepted the trophy and underlined that adverb in the text."

You can use this adverb example when teaching this lesson, or you can create your own example to share with students.

"It's time for you to write. You'll create a passage that uses an adverb, and you'll underline that adverb like I did with my sentence. Then, I'll ask you to share your work with a partner. After that, volunteers will share with the class."

As students create their passages, I recommend circulating the classroom to see how they're doing. I like using this time to praise strong work and provide individualized support.

"Great work creating your examples. Please share with a partner the passage you wrote and identify the adverb you used."

While students share with partners, I like moving through the classroom and listening to them. This is another great time to praise and support students' work.

"I'll now ask for two volunteers to share the passage you wrote and identify the adverb you used."

This time when students share their passage and identify their adverbs is another great opportunity to call attention to strong work and give any needed support.

4. Reflection

At this point in the instructional process, students revisit the passage they created in the writing activity and reflect on the importance of the adverb to that passage.

"In this activity, you'll reread the passage you just created and think about the importance of the adverb you used in that passage. You'll then write an answer to the question 'Why is the adverb you used in your passage important?'"

I suggest displaying this question while reading it aloud to students.

"First, I'll share with you the reflection I wrote about my passage 'She proudly accepted the trophy.' When answering the reflection question, I wrote 'The adverb proudly is important because it explains how the character accepted the trophy. This adverb provides readers with an explanation of the specific way the action discussed in the sentence was performed. If I didn't use it, readers wouldn't know exactly how she accepted the trophy. The explanation provided by the adverb helps readers understand the sentence clearly.'"

If you use this example with your students, I recommend sharing this corresponding reflection. If you create your own passage, I suggest writing and sharing a reflection that aligns with that passage.

"Now, it's time for you to write your reflection. Reread the passage you created that uses an adverb and write an answer to the question 'Why is the adverb you used in your passage important?'"

While students write, I like to walk around the classroom, check on their progress, and provide personalized feedback.

"Nice job responding to the reflection question. Please now share your reflection with a partner and listen as they share theirs with you."

During this time, I suggest listening to what students share and again giving individualized feedback to them.

"We'll now take two volunteers to share their answers to the reflection question with the rest of the class. Afterward, everyone will turn in their reflections along with the passages they created during the writing activity."

When students share their responses with the class, I like to recognize the strengths of their work and elaborate on ideas that can be further enhanced.

5. Exit Question

At the conclusion of this instructional process, students respond to an exit question on the importance of adverbs.

"We'll wrap up our work on adverbs with an exit question. I'll ask you to write an answer to an exit question on adverbs, and I'll ask for two volunteers to share their ideas with the class. Then, I'll collect all of the written responses. The exit question is 'Why are adverbs important tools for strong writing?'"

I recommend displaying the exit question while reading it aloud to students. As volunteers share their responses, I praise strong points and provide clarification and additional explanation when relevant.

Differentiation Suggestions

There are numerous ways this lesson can be differentiated:

- Students can examine additional adverb mentor texts, showing them additional examples of adverbs in published writing.
- Students can read adverb mentor texts on a range of reading levels so they can work with texts that fit them best.
- Students can use more than one adverb in the passages they write.
- Students can write multiple passages that incorporate adverbs.

Assessment

I recommend assessing students' understandings of adverbs and their work in this lesson sequence in two ways:

- Students' exit question responses.
  - The two exit question responses students submit in this lesson sequence can reveal their knowledge of adverbs and the importance of adverbs to strong writing. When assessing students' answers to the first day's exit question, "Why would writers use adverbs in their writing?" I suggest assessing how well students explain that writers use adverbs to provide explanation in their works. When evaluating students' responses to the second day's exit question, "Why are adverbs important

tools for strong writing?" I recommend evaluating if students express that adverbs are important to strong writing because the explanation they give can help readers understand what the author is communicating.
- ◆ Students' written passages and accompanying reflections.
  - The written passages that students create using adverbs and the reflections that go along with those passages are also great ways to assess students' knowledge of this concept. When evaluating students' written passages, I look to see if students used an adverb in their passage, if the adverb provides explanation to the passage, and if that explanation aligns with the piece. When assessing students' answers to the reflection question, I consider the detail and insight they share when discussing the importance of the adverb to the passage.

Notes

- ◆ What worked when teaching this lesson?

- ◆ What might you adapt or change the next time you teach it?

Reference

Chapman, E. (2023). *The scroll of chaos*. Scholastic.

LESSON 3.4

Building Sentences

Simple, Compound, and Complex Sentences

Overview

This lesson focuses on simple, compound, and complex sentences, three sentence types that writers purposefully use in their works. It encompasses two class periods. On day one, students will learn the characteristics of simple, compound, and complex sentences, examine examples of them, see how they are used in published writing, and consider the benefits of their use. On day two, students will review key information about simple, compound, and complex sentences, create examples of each sentence type, and reflect on the benefits of using each one. To conclude the lesson sequence, students will answer an exit question on the importance of simple, compound, and complex sentences to strong writing.

Objectives

- Students will learn the features of simple, compound, and complex sentences.
- Students will understand why simple, compound, and complex sentences are important to strong writing.
- Students will be able to create simple, compound, and complex sentences and reflect on the benefits of using each of these sentence types.

DOI: 10.4324/9781003610656-6

Time Frame

Two class periods.

Background Knowledge Required

Students will need to be familiar with the fundamental features of sentences.

Materials Needed

- Figures 3.4.1–3.4.8. These figures are available in the lesson plan, in Appendix B: Reproducible Graphic Organizers, and on the book's website.
- A board, projector, or piece of chart paper for displaying information.
- Paper for students to use.

Detailed Plan

Day One
1. Introduction

To open this lesson sequence, you'll introduce students to the concepts of simple, compound, and complex sentences, present the key questions students will consider during their first day working on these topics, and share the day's agenda.

"Let's begin our work on simple, compound, and complex sentences, three sentence types that writers use to share information in purposeful ways. We'll focus on these key questions today:

- What are simple, compound, and complex sentences?
- Why are simple, compound, and complex sentences important to strong writing?

Here's our agenda for today's work:

- Mini-lesson on simple, compound, and complex sentences
- Mentor text examples
- Mentor text discussion and analysis activities
- Exit question"

I suggest displaying the day's key questions and items while reading them aloud.

2. Mini-Lesson on Simple, Compound, and Complex Sentences

You'll conduct a mini-lesson on simple, compound, and complex sentences. In it, you'll describe the key features of these sentence types, provide examples of them, and discuss their importance.

"In this mini-lesson on simple, compound, and complex sentences, I'll share key information about these sentence types. This will be the starting point for our work. We'll continue to think about these ideas as we explore simple, compound, and complex sentences.

We'll start by discussing simple sentences. Simple sentences are made up of one independent clause. An independent clause contains a subject and a verb expresses a complete statement. For example, 'Julie played basketball' is an independent clause and is an example of a simple sentence. Simple sentences are important tools for strong writing because they express information directly and clearly. Let's look at a chart that summarizes information about simple sentences."

Sentence Type	Description	Example	Importance to Strong Writing
Simple sentence	A simple sentence is made up of one independent clause.	Julie played basketball.	Simple sentences are important to strong writing because they express information directly and clearly.

Figure 3.4.1 Key Information about Simple Sentences

I recommend displaying this chart and sharing its information out loud.

"Compound sentences contain two or more independent clauses joined by a coordinator. For example, if we turned our simple sentence 'Julie played basketball' into a compound sentence, it could read 'Julie played basketball, and Jeff played soccer.' This sentence contains two independent clauses that are joined by a coordinator. There are different kinds of coordinators we can use in compound sentences. One kind of coordinator is a coordinating conjunction, which can be used with commas to join independent clauses. Coordinating conjunctions are the words *for, and, nor, but, or, yet,* and *so*. For instance, the previously used sentence 'Julie played basketball, and Jeff played soccer' uses a comma and the coordinating conjunction 'and.' Another coordinator often used to link independent clauses in compound sentences is a semicolon. We can use semicolons in place of coordinating conjunctions, such as 'Julie played basketball; Jeff played soccer.' Compound sentences are important tools for strong writing because they connect ideas and help the flow of a piece of writing. Let's check out a chart that highlights ideas about compound sentences."

Sentence Type	Description	Examples	Importance to Strong Writing
Compound sentence	A compound sentence is made up of two or more independent clauses joined by a coordinator, such as a comma and coordinating conjunction or a semicolon.	Julie played basketball, and Jeff played soccer. Julie played basketball; Jeff played soccer.	Compound sentences are important to strong writing because they connect ideas and help the flow of a piece of writing.

Figure 3.4.2 Key Information about Compound Sentences

I suggest projecting this chart and reading its information aloud.

"Complex sentences contain an independent clause and at least one dependent clause. A dependent clause contains a subject and verb, but, unlike an independent clause, cannot stand on its own as a sentence. An example of a complex sentence 'Because she loves the sport, Julie played basketball.' In this sentence, 'Julie played basketball' is an independent clause and 'Because she loves the sport' is a dependent clause. The independent clause can stand on its own as a sentence; the dependent clause can't. Some words that frequently begin dependent clauses are *although, because, if, since, until, after, when,* and *where*. Complex sentences are important tools for strong writing because they include background information and context that helps the reader understand what's taking place. We'll look at information about complex sentences now."

Sentence Type	Description	Example	Importance to Strong Writing
Complex sentence	A complex sentence is made up of an independent clause and at least one dependent clause.	Because she loves the sport, Julie played basketball.	Complex sentences are important to strong writing because the background information and context they provide help the reader understand what's taking place.

Figure 3.4.3 Key Information about Complex Sentences

I recommend displaying this chart and reading its contents for students.

3. Mentor Text Examples

You'll now share with students published examples of simple, compound, and complex sentences. This shows students how these sentence types are used in authentic writing and prepares them for future activities in the lesson.

"Next, we'll look at how published authors use simple, compound, and complex sentences in their writing. I'll share with you published examples of each of these sentence types."

Published Simple Sentence Example	Published Compound Sentence Example	Published Complex Sentence Example
"Her family is really close" (Yee, 2022, p. 1). From *Maizy Chen's Last Chance* by Lisa Yee	"This is my first day of school in America, and things are not going well" (Weeks & Varadarajan, 2016, p. 7). From *Save Me a Seat* by Sarah Weeks and Gita Varadarajan	"If they knew the truth, they would think I was nothing" (Soontornvat, 2022, p. 7). From *The Last Mapmaker* by Christina Soontornvat

Figure 3.4.4 Published Examples of Simple, Compound, and Complex Sentences

I recommend displaying these sentences and reading them aloud. While reading them, I like talking with students about why each sentence is an example of its type.

4. Mentor Text Discussion and Analysis Activities

Next, you'll lead students through activities that will help them understand the benefits associated with using each of the sentence types found in the mentor text examples.

"Now that we've seen published examples of simple, compound, and complex sentences, we'll discuss the benefits of using each of these sentence types. We'll re-examine each mentor text example, and you'll think about the benefits of using that sentence type. First, I'll display our simple sentence example. Next, you'll talk with a partner about the benefits of using that simple sentence. Then, we'll record some responses in the chart I'll display."

Simple Sentence Mentor Text	Benefits of Using This Sentence Type
"Her family is really close" (Yee, 2022, p. 1).	

Figure 3.4.5 Simple Sentence Benefits Analysis Chart

I suggest displaying this chart, reading the sentence aloud, and asking students to talk with partners about some benefits of using a simple sentence in this situation. While students talk, I like to move around the room to listen to and support them. Then, I ask for volunteers to share ideas and record them on the chart. When students share, I look for responses that highlight how the simple sentence allows the writer to express information clearly and directly.

"Next, we'll think about our compound sentence mentor text. I'll display the compound sentence example and ask you to talk with a partner about the benefits of using that sentence type. We'll then record some responses on the chart."

Compound Sentence Mentor Text	Benefits of Using This Sentence Type
"This is my first day of school in America, and things are not going well" (Weeks & Varadarajan, 2016, p. 7).	

Figure 3.4.6 Compound Sentence Benefits Analysis Chart

I recommend displaying this information, reading aloud the sentence, and then asking student pairs to discuss the benefits of using a compound sentence in this situation. I circulate the classroom while students talk, listening to and supporting their work. I then record on the chart ideas that volunteers share. When students share, I especially look for comments that explain how the compound sentence connects ideas and helps the flow of the sentence.

"We'll now focus on our complex sentence mentor text. We'll look at the complex sentence example. Then, you'll talk to a partner about the benefits of using that sentence type. I'll write some responses on this chart."

Complex Sentence Mentor Text	**Benefits of Using This Sentence Type**
"If they knew the truth, they would think I was nothing" (Soontornvat, 2022, p. 7).	

Figure 3.4.7 Complex Sentence Benefits Analysis Chart

You'll share this chart with students, read the example aloud, and ask students to talk with partners about the benefits of a complex sentence in this situation. While students talk, I recommend circulating the classroom and providing any needed assistance. After that, I ask volunteers to share, recording insights on the chart. I look for responses that highlight how the complex sentence helps the author provide background information that can be useful to readers.

5. Exit Question

To conclude this class period, students answer an exit question about simple, compound, and complex sentences.

"Now, you'll write an answer to an exit question about simple, compound, and complex sentences. After that, I'll ask for two volunteers to share, and I'll collect everyone's answers. The exit question is 'Why would writers use simple, compound, and complex sentences in their writing?'"

I like to display this question while students write their answers. After students submit their responses, I examine their answers to evaluate their understandings and use that evaluation to inform future instruction.

Day Two
1. Introduction
To begin the second day on simple, compound, and complex sentences, you'll explain how students' work that day will build on the previous one, share the day's questions, and present the agenda.

"Great work yesterday on simple, compound, and complex sentences! You learned about these sentence types, examined published examples of them, reflected on the benefits of the published authors using each one, and answered an exit question about why writers use these sentence types in their writing. Today, we'll work with these sentence types even more. We'll review key information about them, create our own examples of each sentence type, reflect on the benefits of using each one, and answer an exit question on the importance of simple, compound, and complex sentences to strong writing. Today's key questions are:

- How can we use simple, compound, and complex sentences in our writing?
- How does our writing benefit from using these sentence types?

Here is today's agenda:

- Review of simple, compound, and complex sentences
- Writing activity
- Reflection
- Exit question"

I suggest displaying the key questions and agenda while sharing them with students.

2. Review of Simple, Compound, and Complex Sentences
You'll review key information about simple, compound, and complex sentences, highlighting significant ideas discussed the previous day.

"Let's review important information about simple, compound, and complex sentences by looking at a review chart. It provides the following information about each sentence type: a description of it, the published example we saw in our last class, and information about its importance to strong writing."

Sentence Type	Description	Published Example	Importance to Strong Writing
Simple sentence	A simple sentence is made up of one independent clause.	"Her family is really close" (Yee, 2022, p. 1).	Simple sentences are important to strong writing because they express information directly and clearly.
Compound sentence	A compound sentence is made up of two or more independent clauses joined by a coordinator, such as a comma and coordinating conjunction or a semicolon.	"This is my first day of school in America, and things are not going well" (Weeks & Varadarajan, 2016, p. 7).	Compound sentences are important to strong writing because they connect ideas and help the flow of a piece of writing.
Complex sentence	A complex sentence is made up of an independent clause and at least one dependent clause.	"If they knew the truth, they would think I was nothing" (Soontornvat, 2022, p. 7).	Complex sentences are important to strong writing because the background information and context they provide help the reader understand what's taking place.

Figure 3.4.8 Simple, Compound, and Complex Sentence Review Information

I suggest projecting this chart, reading its contents aloud, and discussing questions students have about these sentence types.

3. Writing Activity

Students now apply their knowledge of simple, compound, and complex sentences to their writing by creating examples of each of these sentence types.

"Now, we'll write our own examples of these sentence types! You'll create a simple sentence, a compound sentence, and a complex sentence. Before you write, I'll share the examples I created. My simple sentence is 'The students celebrated.' My compound sentence is 'The students celebrated, and the teachers cheered.' My complex sentence is 'Because they won an award, the students celebrated.' When you create your own sentences, you can make them about similar topics like I did, but you can also make them about different topics. It's up to you!"

You can use these same examples or create your own to share with students.

"You'll create your own examples of simple, compound, and complex sentences. I'll check in with you while you work."

As students create sentences, I suggest circulating the classroom, monitoring their progress, and providing relevant praise and support.

"Good job working on those sentences! Let's take two volunteers to share the sentences they created and identify the sentence types."

When students share their sentences, I recommend praising strong examples of these sentence types and providing any needed clarification.

4. Reflection

Here, students revisit the sentences they created in the writing activity and reflect on the benefits of using each sentence type.

"We're going to do a reflective activity with the sentences you just wrote. You'll re-read your sentences and then answer the following question for each sentence you wrote: 'What is a benefit of using that sentence type?'"

I recommend displaying this question for students.

"Before you do this, I'll share my reflections on the sentences I created. For the simple sentence 'The students celebrated,' I said, 'A benefit of using this simple sentence is that the sentence shares information about the students celebrating clearly and directly.' For the compound sentence 'The students celebrated, and the teachers cheered,' I reflected, 'A benefit of using a compound sentence here is that it connects information about the students and teachers.' For the complex sentence 'Because they won an award, the students celebrated,' I wrote, 'A benefit of using this complex sentence is that the sentence gives background information that helps readers understand why the students celebrated.'"

If you use these examples, you can share this reflection with students. If you create your own examples, you can share a reflection that aligns with them.

"Look back at the simple, compound, and complex sentences you wrote and answer the question 'What is a benefit of using that sentence type?' for each."

While students write, I circulate the classroom to provide support and encouragement.

"Let's now have two volunteers share their sentences and reflections verbally. Then, everyone will turn in their sentences and reflections."

When students share, I suggest identifying strong points and clarifying any confusion.

5. Exit Question

This sequence ends with an exit question on the importance of simple, compound, and complex sentences.

"We'll finish with an exit question on simple, compound, and complex sentences. You'll write your answers, two volunteers will share, and I'll collect them. The exit question is 'Why are simple, compound, and complex sentences important tools for strong writing?'"

I suggest displaying this question. When students answer, I praise strong statements and provide any needed explanation.

Differentiation Suggestions

This lesson can be differentiated in several ways:

- Students can examine additional mentor text examples of simple, compound, and complex sentences.
- Students can read examples of these sentence types on a variety of reading levels.
- Students can write multiple examples of these sentence types.

Assessment

I suggest assessing students' knowledge of simple, compound, and complex sentences in these ways:

- Students' exit question responses.
    - Students' responses to the exit questions in this instructional process provide insights into their knowledge of simple, compound, and complex sentences. When assessing students' responses to the day-one question, "Why would writers use simple, compound, and complex sentences in their writing?," I evaluate how well students explain that writers use these sentence types purposefully to achieve the benefits that each one provides. When evaluating students' responses to the day-two exit question, "Why are simple, compound, and complex sentences important tools for strong writing?," I look at how well students explain that each of these sentences is important in its own way.

- Students' written examples and reflections.
  - The examples that students create and their corresponding reflections also provide important assessment data. I assess students' sentences to determine if they accurately created examples of each sentence type. I evaluate students' reflections to assess if they understand the benefits of each type.

Notes

- What worked when teaching this lesson?

- What might you adapt or change the next time you teach it?

References

Soontornvat, C. (2022). *The last mapmaker*. Candlewick Press.

Weeks, S., & Varadarajan, G. (2016). *Save me a seat*. Scholastic.

Yee, L. (2022). *Maizy Chen's last chance*. Random House Books for Young Readers.

LESSON 3.5

In Dialogue

Using Commas and Quotation Marks When Writing Dialogue

Overview

This lesson addresses how writers use commas and quotation marks when writing dialogue, an important tactic for clearly identifying a speaker's words in a piece of writing. The lesson spans two class periods. On day one, students will learn what it means to use commas (when needed) and quotation marks when writing dialogue, see examples of how writers do this, explore published mentor texts of this concept, and consider its impact. On day two, students will review this concept, apply it to their writing, and reflect on the significance of using commas (when needed) and quotation marks when writing dialogue. At the conclusion of this instructional process, students will consider how this concept can be important to their future writing.

Objectives

- Students will understand the concept of using commas and quotation marks when writing dialogue.
- Students will understand the importance of using commas (when needed) and quotation marks in strong writing.
- Students will be able to use commas (when needed) and quotation marks when writing dialogue in their works and reflect on the importance of doing so.

Time Frame

Two class periods.

Background Knowledge Required

Students will need to know what commas and quotation marks are.

Materials Needed

- Figures 3.5.1–3.5.7. They are available in the lesson plan, in Appendix B: Reproducible Graphic Organizers, and in electronic format on the book's website.
- A board, projector, or piece of chart paper for displaying information.
- Paper for students' writing activities.

Detailed Plan

Day One
1. Introduction

You'll begin this instructional process by introducing students to the concept of using commas and quotation marks when writing dialogue, sharing the key questions they'll investigate on their first day working on the topic, and presenting the day's agenda.

"Today, we'll explore the grammatical concept of using commas (when needed) and quotation marks when writing dialogue. We'll examine these questions:

- What does it mean to use commas (when needed) and quotation marks when writing dialogue?
- What are some ways that this concept can look in writing?
- Why is using commas (when needed) and quotation marks when writing dialogue important to strong writing?

Here is the agenda for today's work:

- Mini-lesson on using commas and quotation marks when writing dialogue
- Mentor text examples

- Mentor text discussion and analysis activities
- Exit question"

I suggest displaying these questions and agenda items while reading them aloud.

2. Mini-Lesson on Using Commas and Quotation Marks When Writing Dialogue

In this mini-lesson, you'll introduce students to the concept of using commas and quotation marks when writing dialogue, describe the concept's importance, discuss forms it can take in writing, and provide examples of these forms.

"It's time for our mini-lesson on using commas and quotation marks when writing dialogue, which is our first step together exploring this concept. Let's start with what this concept is. When writing dialogue, writers use the punctuation marks of commas (when needed) and quotation marks to show what a speaker is saying. This concept is important to strong writing because it allows writers to clearly separate a speaker's words from the rest of the piece. If a writer didn't use these punctuation marks when writing dialogue when they're needed, readers wouldn't be able to tell which part of the text was dialogue and which part was not. There are four typical ways writers use commas (when needed) and quotation marks when writing dialogue. The differences between them have to do with something called a speaker tag, which, when it's used, is the part of the sentence that identifies the speaker, such as 'Joe said.' We're going to look together at a chart that summarizes key information about using commas and quotation marks when writing dialogue. It also contains examples of four key ways that writers use this concept in writing."

Grammatical Concept	What Is It?	Why Is It Important to Strong Writing?	What Are Examples of How It's Used?
Using commas and quotation marks when writing dialogue.	When writing dialogue, writers use the punctuation marks of commas (when needed) and quotation marks to show what a speaker is saying.	This concept is important to strong writing because it allows writers to clearly separate a speaker's words from the rest of the piece.	Example One: The Speaker Tag Comes Before the Quotation: Joe said, "I want to see a manatee."

Figure 3.5.1 Information and Examples Regarding Using Commas and Quotation Marks When Writing Dialogue

(Continued)

Grammatical Concept	What Is It?	Why Is It Important to Strong Writing?	What Are Examples of How It's Used?
			Example Two: The Speaker Tag Follows the Quotation: "I want to see a manatee," Joe said. Example Three: The Speaker Tag Interrupts the Quotation: "I want," Joe said, "to see a manatee." Example Four: There Is No Speaker Tag: "I want to see a manatee."

Figure 3.5.1 (Continued)

I recommend projecting this chart while sharing its contents with students. When talking with students about the examples, I suggest pointing out where the dialogue is in each sentence and calling **attention** *to how the relevant commas (when needed) and quotation marks separate the quoted text from the rest of the sentence. It's important to note that in example four, there are no commas used with the quotation marks because there is no speaker tag to separate from the rest of the sentence. By pointing this out, you'll show students the difference between this pattern and the other three that combine commas with quotation marks.*

3. Mentor Text Examples

You'll now share with students published sentences in which authors used commas (when needed) and quotation marks when writing dialogue. These examples show students how this concept is used in authentic writing.

"Let's now look at how published authors use commas (when needed) and quotation marks when writing dialogue in their works. I'll share with you published versions of each of the examples we discussed in our mini-lesson."

Example One: The Speaker Tag Comes Before the Quotation	Example Two: The Speaker Tag Follows the Quotation	Example Three: The Speaker Tag Interrupts the Quotation	Example Four: There Is No Speaker Tag
He looked at Grandma and said, "Iris has gotten used to her school" (Kelly, 2019, p. 51).	"He's probably left already," said Josie (Raúf, 2018, p. 17).	"You know," she began, "I had a dream about the Stone Boy again last night" (Kelly, 2017, p. 5).	"Can I have it?" (Pennypacker, 2016, p. 9).

Figure 3.5.2 Published Examples of Sentences That Use Commas (When Needed) and Quotation Marks to Show Dialogue

I suggest displaying these sentences and reading them aloud. As with the examples in Figure 3.5.1, I recommend identifying the dialogue in each sentence and pointing out how the relevant commas (when needed) and quotation marks separate the quoted text from the rest of the sentence.

4. Mentor Text Discussion and Analysis Activities

This part of the lesson helps students think about the importance of commas (when needed) and quotation marks used to indicate dialogue in the mentor text examples.

"Now that we've looked at these examples of published texts that use commas (when needed) and quotation marks when writing dialogue, we'll explore why this punctuation is important to these tests. We'll compare each published example with a new version that doesn't contain commas (when needed) and quotation marks to show what the speaker is saying. After that, we'll discuss the importance of those punctuation marks."

I recommend displaying Figure 3.5.3 and talking with students about how the comma after "said" and the quotation marks surrounding the quote are important because they let readers know exactly what the speaker said and separate this information from the speaker tag that comes before the quotation. While you conduct this discussion, I suggest recording highlights of the conversation in the right-hand column.

Mentor Text Example	Example Without Comma and Quotation Marks That Shows Dialogue	Why This Punctuation Is Important to the Sentence
He looked at Grandma and said, "Iris has gotten used to her school" (Kelly, 2019, p. 51).	He looked at Grandma and said Iris has gotten used to her school.	

Figure 3.5.3 Mentor Text Discussion Chart. Example One: The Speaker Tag Comes Before the Quotation

Next, I suggest displaying Figure 3.5.4 and discussing with students that the quotation marks surrounding the quote and the comma after "already" are important to the sentence because they clearly separate Josie's quotation from the speaker tag that follows it. I recommend recording key points from this discussion in the right-hand column.

Mentor Text Example	Example Without Comma and Quotation Marks That Shows Dialogue	Why This Punctuation Is Important to the Sentence
"He's probably left already," said Josie (Raúf, 2018, p. 17).	He's probably left already said Josie.	

Figure 3.5.4 Mentor Text Discussion Chart. Example Two: The Speaker Tag Follows the Quotation

After that, I like to show students Figure 3.5.5, which features a mentor text that uses commas and quotation marks to show that the speaker tag interrupts the quotation. I like to talk with students about how the quotation marks and the commas after "know" and before "I" are important to the sentence because they clearly separate the speaker tag that interrupts the quotation from the quotation itself. During this discussion, I like to record highlights in the right-hand column.

Mentor Text Example	Example Without Commas and Quotation Marks That Shows Dialogue	Why This Punctuation Is Important to the Sentence
"You know," she began, "I had a dream about the Stone Boy again last night" (Kelly, 2017, p. 5).	You know she began I had a dream about the Stone Boy again last night.	

Figure 3.5.5 Mentor Text Discussion Chart. Example Three: The Speaker Tag Interrupts the Quotation

To conclude this activity, I recommend showing students Figure 3.5.6, which contains a quotation mentor text that does not include a speaker tag. I suggest talking with students about how the quotation marks are important because they show that the text in the sentence is a direct quotation. I also recommend calling attention to the fact that this example is different from the others because it does not contain a speaker tag and therefore does not use any commas to set that speaker tag apart from the rest of the sentence like the other examples do. As you talk with students about the importance of quotation marks, I suggest recording key ideas in the right-hand column.

Mentor Text Example	Example Without Quotation Marks That Shows Dialogue	Why This Punctuation Is Important to the Sentence
"Can I have it?" (Pennypacker, 2016, p. 9).	Can I have it?	

Figure 3.5.6 Mentor Text Discussion Chart. Example Three: There Is No Speaker Tag

5. Exit Question

This exit question asks students to reflect on key information they learned that day about using commas and quotation marks when writing dialogue.

"Now you'll write an answer to an exit question about using commas and quotation marks when writing dialogue. I'll then ask for two volunteers to share and collect everyone's answers. The exit question is 'Why do writers use commas (when needed) and quotation marks when writing dialogue?'"

I suggest displaying this question while students write answers. I evaluate students' responses to assess their understanding and use this information to inform my future instruction.

Day Two
1. Introduction

To introduce this second day of instruction on using commas and quotation marks when writing dialogue, you'll tell students how they'll build on their previous work on this topic, present the day's key questions, and share the agenda.

"Great job yesterday working on the topic of using commas and quotation marks when writing dialogue! We discussed the uses of commas (when needed) and quotation marks when writing dialogue to show what the speaker is saying, looked at published examples, analyzed the importance of these punctuation marks to those examples, and answered an exit question on this topic. Today, we'll build on this work. We'll start by reviewing information about this topic, and then we'll use this grammatical concept in our writing. After that, we'll reflect on the significance of using it in our works. We'll end with an exit question about how we'll use commas (when needed) and quotation marks when writing dialogue in our future works. Today's key questions are:

- How can we use commas (when needed) and quotation marks when writing dialogue in our writing?
- Why is using commas (when needed) and quotation marks when writing dialogue important to our writing?

Here's today's agenda:

- Review of using commas and quotation marks when writing dialogue
- Writing application
- Reflection
- Exit question"

I recommend displaying this information while sharing it.

2. Review of Using Commas and Quotation Marks When Writing Dialogue

In this part of the lesson, you'll review the information you shared in the previous day's opening mini-lesson about the concept of using commas and quotation marks when writing dialogue, addressing what this topic is, why it's important, and examples of its use.

"Let's get started by reviewing key information about using commas and quotation marks when writing dialogue. I'll share with you the chart we looked at in yesterday's mini-lesson that explains what using commas and quotation marks when writing dialogue is, describing why it's important to strong writing, and providing examples of its use."

To review this information about using commas and quotation marks when writing dialogue, I suggest displaying Figure 3.5.1 and reviewing the information that the chart provides about what this concept is, why it's important to strong writing, and how examples of it can look. During this time, I also suggest further discussing any aspects of this topic about which students have shown confusion.

3. Writing Activity

In this activity, students create a sentence that uses commas (if needed) and quotation marks when writing an example of dialogue. They will choose one of the sentence structures to use when writing this example.

"Now, we're going to use our knowledge of using commas and quotation marks when writing dialogue in a writing activity. You can use any of the four example structures that we've seen in our work on this topic. Before you start, I'll share an example I created, which I'll write on the board."

Bill said, "You can borrow my book."

You can use this same example or create your own to share with students.

"In this sentence, the speaker tag 'Bill said' comes before the quotation. Because of this, there is a comma between the speaker tag and the quotation. The quotation marks go around 'You can borrow my book' because that's what Bill said. Now, it's your turn! Create your own example of a sentence that uses commas (if needed) and quotation marks when writing dialogue. Remember that you can use any of the four example structures we've seen. I'll check in with you while you work."

As students write, I suggest moving around the classroom to check in on their progress and provide support and praise.

"Good job creating those examples! Let's have two volunteers share. Each volunteer will share their sentence, identify the kind of example they used, and talk about how they used commas (if needed) and quotation marks when writing the dialogue."

When students share and discuss their work, I like to praise strong examples and explanations. In addition, I recommend providing any clarification or further explanation if needed.

4. Reflection

During this next step of the lesson, students take the sentences they wrote during the writing activity, rewrite them without commas (if applicable) and quotation marks that show dialogue, and reflect on the differences between those sentences.

"In this next activity, you'll return to the piece of writing you just created, rewrite it without the commas (if you used any) and the quotation marks you used to show what a speaker is saying, and then write a brief reflection on why the punctuation you used to show dialogue is important to the sentence. This graphic organizer will help you organize your work in this activity."

Your Original Passage	Revised Version Without the Commas (If Any) and Quotation Marks That Shows Dialogue	Why the Punctuation You Used to Show Dialogue Is Important to the Sentence

Figure 3.5.7 Reflection Graphic Organizer

I recommend displaying this chart while reading its contents aloud. When students complete the activity, I suggest making copies of the chart for them, providing them with electronic examples, or asking them to recreate the chart in their notebooks.

"Before you start, I'll show you my example. I'll write my original passage in the graphic organizer."

Bill said, "You can borrow my book."

If you use this same example, I recommend writing it in the graphic organizer in Figure 3.5.7 and displaying that information. If you use a different example, please write that one instead.

"Now, I'll write how that passage would look without the comma and quotation marks that show dialogue."

Bill said You can borrow my book.

If you are using this same example, I suggest writing this text in the graphic organizer. If you are using a different example, I suggest writing that text without any commas (if needed) and quotation marks that show dialogue.

"Finally, I'll write why I think the punctuation I used to show dialogue is important to the sentence. I'll write 'The comma after said and the quotation marks before the word you and after the word book are important because they show that the exact language that Bill said was you can borrow my book. Without this punctuation, it wouldn't be clear that this was exactly what Bill said.'"

If you are using this example, I recommend sharing this explanation or another one like it. If you use a different example, I recommend providing an explanation that aligns with the example you share.

"Now, it's your turn! You'll use the graphic organizer to write your original passage, share a revised version without the commas (if any) and quotation marks that show dialogue, and write a reflection about why the punctuation you used to show dialogue is important to the sentence. I'll check in with you while you work."

I like to circulate the classroom while students work, giving them individualized suggestions and praise.

"Excellent work on this activity! I'll now ask for two volunteers to share. Each volunteer will share their original sentence, say what punctuation they removed in the revised version, and explain why the punctuation that shows dialogue is important to the sentence. After that, everyone will turn in the sentence they created during the writing activity and the graphic organizer they completed during this activity."

When students share their work, I recommend calling attention to especially strong reflections. If any statements can be further developed, I suggest providing any needed explanation or clarification.

5. Exit Question

At the conclusion of this instructional process, students answer an exit question about using commas (when needed) and quotation marks when writing dialogue.

"We'll conclude our work with an exit question on using commas (when needed) and quotation marks when writing dialogue. After you write an answer to the exit question, two volunteers will share their responses, and then I'll collect everyone's written answers. The exit question is 'How can using commas (when needed) and quotation marks when writing dialogue be important to your future writing?'"

I suggest displaying this question while reading it. As students share, I like to praise the strong insights and ideas they provide.

Differentiation Suggestions

This lesson can be differentiated in a variety of ways:

- Students can examine additional mentor text examples of sentences that use commas (when needed) and quotation marks to show dialogue to give them additional exposure to published uses of this topic.
- Students can engage with mentor texts on a variety of reading levels so they can read examples that best fit them.
- Students can create multiple examples of sentences that use commas (when needed) and quotation marks when writing dialogue.
- Students can create examples that represent different ways to use commas (when needed) and quotation marks when writing dialogue.

Assessment

I suggest assessing students' knowledge of using commas and quotation marks to show dialogue and their work in this lesson sequence in two ways:

- Students' exit question responses.
  - The exit question responses students create during this instructional process provide important insight into their knowledge of using commas and quotation marks to show dialogue. When evaluating students' work on the day-one exit question, "Why do writers use commas (when needed) and quotation marks when writing dialogue?" I suggest assessing how well students explain that writers use this strategy to clearly separate a speaker's words from the rest of the piece. When assessing students' responses to the day-two exit question, "How can using commas (when needed) and quotation marks when writing dialogue be important to your future writing?" I recommend evaluating how well students explain that they can use this tactic in their future works to help readers identify a speaker's words in their writing.
- Students' written examples and reflections.
  - I recommend assessing students' understanding of using commas (when needed) and quotation marks to show dialogue by reading the examples they created during the writing activity

and the corresponding reflections they shared on the graphic organizer depicted in Figure 3.5.7. When evaluating students' work on the writing activity, I look to see which of the structures they used and if they correctly used commas (if needed) and quotation marks to show dialogue in their example. When assessing students' reflections, I consider the detail and insight they provided when describing why the punctuation they used to show dialogue is important to their sentences.

Notes

◆ What worked when teaching this lesson?

◆ What might you adapt or change the next time you teach it?

References

Kelly, E.E. (2017). *Hello, universe*. Greenwillow Books.
Kelly, L. (2019). *Song for a whale*. Yearling.
Pennypacker, S. (2016). *Pax*. Balzer + Bray.
Raúf, O.Q. (2018). *The boy at the back of the class*. Yearling.

SECTION TWO

Lesson Plans Recommended for the Fourth-Grade Classroom

LESSON 4.1

A Big Deal

Capitalization

Overview

This lesson focuses on the grammatical concept of capitalization, addressing key ideas regarding capitalization use and discussing the significance of this topic. The lesson spans two class periods. On the first day, students will learn key capitalization rules, see examples of them, consider their importance, explore how published writers use them, and think about their impact on writing. On the second day, students will review capitalization-related ideas and information, apply key capitalization concepts to their own writing, and reflect on the significance of doing so. To conclude the instructional process, students will answer an exit question about the importance of capitalization to strong writing.

Objectives

- Students will understand key ideas regarding the use of capitalization.
- Students will understand the importance of capitalization to strong writing.
- Students will be able to apply key capitalization rules to their writing and reflect on the importance of doing so.

DOI: 10.4324/9781003610656-9

Time Frame

Two class periods.

Background Knowledge Required

Students need background knowledge regarding proper nouns.

Materials Needed

- Figures 4.1.1–4.1.5, which are available in the lesson plan, in Appendix B: Reproducible Graphic Organizers, and on the book's website.
- A board, projector, or piece of chart paper for displaying information.
- Paper for students to use.

Detailed Plan

Day One
1. Introduction

You'll introduce this instructional process by letting students know that they'll be studying capitalization, presenting the key questions about capitalization the class will explore that day, and sharing the day's agenda.

"We're going to explore the grammatical concept of capitalization. We'll learn important information about capitalizing letters in writing. Today, we'll think about these questions today:

- What are key ideas about capitalizing letters in writing?
- Why do writers use capitalization in their works?

Now, let's look at today's agenda, which lists the activities we'll do as we learn about capitalization:

- Capitalization mini-lesson
- Mentor text examples
- Mentor text discussion and analysis activities
- Exit question"

I recommend displaying the day's questions and agenda items while reading them aloud to students.

2. Capitalization Mini-Lesson

In this mini-lesson on capitalization, you'll share information about capitalization, share key capitalization rules, provide examples of those rules in action, and discuss the importance of capitalization.

"I'm going to share ideas and information about capitalization in this mini-lesson. This will be the starting point for our work on this topic. Capitalization is the use of capital, or uppercase, letters when writing. This concept is important to strong writing because it makes writing clear and helps readers understand a piece of writing without being distracted by capitalization mistakes. Let's look at a chart that contains information about what capitalization is and why it's important."

Grammatical Concept	What Is Capitalization?	Why Is Capitalization Important to Strong Writing?
Capitalization	Capitalization is the use of capital, or uppercase letters, when writing.	Capitalization is important to strong writing because it makes writing clear and helps readers understand a piece of writing without being distracted by capitalization mistakes.

Figure 4.1.1 Capitalization Information

I recommend displaying this chart while reading its information aloud.

"There are key rules about capitalization that we'll discuss. We'll now look at a chart that describes key rules about capitalization and provides examples of those rules in action."

Capitalization Rule	Example
Capitalize the first letter of the first word in a sentence.	**We** are going to the party.
Capitalize the pronoun *I*.	**I** am outside.
Capitalize proper nouns.	We traveled to **Boston**.

Figure 4.1.2 Key Capitalization Rules and Examples

(Continued)

Capitalization Rule	Example
Capitalize titles that come before names.	They met **Mayor Smith.**
Capitalize days of the week, months of the year, and holidays.	**Thanksgiving** takes place on a **Thursday** in **November.**
Capitalize the names of countries, nationalities, and specific languages.	She likes to visit **Canada.**

Figure 4.1.2 (Continued)

I suggest displaying this chart, reading the rules and examples to students, and explaining the examples.

3. Mentor Text Examples

Now, you'll share with students published examples of each of the capitalization rules identified in the mini-lesson. This will show students how these capitalization rules are used authentically in writing.

"Let's now look at published examples of the capitalization rules we explored in the mini-lesson. I'm going to display a chart that contains published examples of each of these rules."

Capitalization Rule	Published Example
Capitalize the first letter of the first word in a sentence.	"**She** crept forward along the wall" (Beatty, 2015, p. 4). From *Serafina and the Black Cloak* by Robert Beatty
Capitalize the pronoun *I*.	"Dad and **I** jump" (Thomas, 2023, p. 4). From *Nic Blake and the Remarkables: The Manifestor Prophecy* by Angie Thomas
Capitalize proper nouns.	"We held hands and leaned to the left to watch **New York** come in closer" (Williams-Garcia, 2013, p. 2). From *P.S. Be Eleven* by Rita Williams-Garcia
Capitalize titles that come before names.	"You should give **Cousin** Lucretia a ring" (Johnson, 2018, p. 42). From *The Parker Inheritance* by Varian Johnson

Figure 4.1.3 Published Examples of Capitalization Rules

(Continued)

Capitalization Rule	Published Example
Capitalize days of the week, months of the year, and holidays.	"Anna and I dressed up as salt and pepper shakers for **Halloween**" (Franklin, 2015, p. 2). From *Extraordinary* by Miriam Spitzer Franklin
Capitalize the names of countries, nationalities, and specific languages.	"Not even a **Chinese** restaurant" (O'Connor, 2016, p. 6). From *Wish* by Barbara O'Connor

Figure 4.1.3 (Continued)

I recommend displaying this chart and reading its contents to students as they follow along. While doing so, I point out the capitalized word in bold in each published example and explain to students why that word represents the capitalization rule that it does.

4. Mentor Text Discussion and Analysis Activities

In this section of the lesson, students will work together to analyze the importance of the published examples of capitalization rules they saw in the last activity.

"Now that we've seen published examples of our capitalization rules, we're going to work together to analyze why those examples of capitalization are so important to the books in which they were used. I'm going to show you a chart that contains the published examples we saw in our last activity compared with how those sentences would look if certain words in those examples were not capitalized. The chart also contains a space to record ideas about why the capitalization in the original example is important. After we look together at the chart, we'll work in groups to analyze the importance of the capitalization in the original examples, and I'll record your ideas."

Published Example	Written without Key Capitalization Rule Used	Why the Capitalization in the Original Example Is Important
"**She** crept forward along the wall" (Beatty, 2015, p. 4). From *Serafina and the Black Cloak* by Robert Beatty	she crept forward along the wall.	

Figure 4.1.4 Mentor Text Comparison and Discussion Chart

(Continued)

Published Example	Written without Key Capitalization Rule Used	Why the Capitalization in the Original Example Is Important
"Dad and I jump" (Thomas, 2023, p. 4). From *Nic Blake and the Remarkables: The Manifestor Prophecy* by Angie Thomas	Dad and i jump.	
"We held hands and leaned to the left to watch **New York** come in closer" (Williams-Garcia, 2013, p. 2). From *P.S. Be Eleven* by Rita Williams-Garcia	We held hands and leaned to the left to watch new york come in closer.	
"You should give **Cousin** Lucretia a ring" (Johnson, 2018, p. 42). From *The Parker Inheritance* by Varian Johnson	You should give cousin Lucretia a ring.	
"Anna and I dressed up as salt and pepper shakers for **Halloween**" (Franklin, 2015, p. 2). From *Extraordinary* by Miriam Spitzer Franklin	Anna and I dressed up as salt and pepper shakers for halloween.	
"Not even a **Chinese** restaurant" (O'Connor, 2016, p. 6). From *Wish* by Barbara O'Connor	Not even a chinese restaurant.	

Figure 4.1.4 (Continued)

I recommend displaying this chart and pointing out the capitalization rule that is present in each original sentence and not used in the corresponding revised version. After that, I suggest asking students to work in groups to discuss and analyze why the capitalization in each original example is important to the sentence. I like to divide the class into six groups and give each group a sentence to analyze. While students work on this activity, I move around the classroom to provide any support they need. Once students have completed their group analyses, I ask each group to share its thoughts with the class. I then record highlights from their responses on the chart, identifying strong insights and providing elaboration and clarification when relevant.

5. Exit Question

To conclude this class period, students answer an exit question that asks them to reflect on capitalization.

"We'll finish our work on capitalization today with an exit question on this topic. Please write your answer to the exit question on a piece of paper. After you write, I'll ask for two volunteers to share, and I'll collect everyone's responses. The exit question is 'Why do writers use capitalization in their works?'"

I recommend displaying this question while you read it and students write their answers. After students submit their answers, I read their work to evaluate their understandings. I then use this evaluation to inform my upcoming instruction on capitalization.

Day Two
1. Introduction

You'll begin the second day of work on capitalization by telling students how the work they'll do will build on the previous day's lesson, providing the day's focal questions, and sharing the agenda.

"Great work yesterday on capitalization! In our work yesterday, we discussed what capitalization is, why it's important to strong writing, and key capitalization rules and examples. After that, we looked at published examples of these capitalization rules and analyzed why the capitalization rules are important to the published examples before ending with an exit question about why writers use capitalization. Today, we'll go into even more depth with capitalization. First, we'll review important capitalization information. Then, we'll create our own written works that use key capitalization rules and reflect on the importance of using those rules. After that, we'll consider why capitalization is an important tool for strong writing. Our key questions for today are:

- How can we use key capitalization rules in our writing?
- Why is capitalization an important tool for strong writing?

Here's our agenda for today:

- Capitalization review
- Writing activity
- Reflection
- Exit question"

I suggest displaying the key questions and agenda items while presenting them to students.

2. Capitalization Review

Here, you'll review the information you shared in the previous day's mini-lesson about capitalization, its importance to effective writing, key capitalization rules, and examples of those rules.

"We'll get started on today's work by reviewing important information about capitalization. First, I'll share with you the chart we looked at yesterday that describes what capitalization is and discusses its importance to strong writing."

At this stage, you'll display Figure 4.1.1, which you shared in the previous day's mini-lesson. This chart contains information about what capitalization is and why it's important to strong writing. As you share this chart, I suggest describing the information and emphasizing any points that you feel can benefit students.

Next, you'll project Figure 4.1.2, which you also shared the preceding day. It contains key capitalization rules and examples of the uses of those rules. While discussing the information in the chart, I recommend providing extra clarification and explanation regarding anything that students showed confusion about in the previous class.

3. Writing Activity

In this activity, students create written passages that use at least two of the capitalization rules they've learned. This allows them to put their capitalization knowledge into action in their writing.

"We're now going to apply our knowledge of capitalization rules to our own writing. You'll write a passage one or two sentences long that uses at least two of the capitalization rules that we've talked about. After you write your passages, you'll share your example with a partner and tell them which capitalization rules you used. Before you start, I'll share an example I created, which I'll write on the board."

"They love to dress up on Halloween."

You can use this same example or create a new one to share with students.

"In this sentence, I capitalized the first letter of 'They' and the first letter of 'Halloween.' I capitalized the 'T' in 'They' because 'They' is the first word of the sentence. I capitalized the 'H' in 'Halloween' because 'Halloween' is a holiday. Now, it's your turn! Create your own passage of one or two sentences that uses at least two of the capitalization rules we've talked about."

While students write, I like to move around the classroom, checking in on them and providing support and praise.

"Great work creating those examples. We'll now have two volunteers share. Each volunteer will share their passage, identify the words they capitalized, and say which capitalization rule each capitalized word relates to."

As students share their work, I suggest praising strong examples and providing any additional explanation that can support students. If students are confused about any capitalization concepts, I provide any needed clarification.

4. Reflection

During this reflective activity, students take the passages they wrote in the last part of the lesson, rewrite them without the capitalization rules they used, and reflect on why the capitalization rules are important to the original sentence.

"In our next activity, you'll revisit the passage you just created, write it down, rewrite it without the capitalization rules you used, and then write a brief reflection on why the capitalization in the original passage is important. This graphic organizer will help you organize your work on the activity."

Your Original Passage	Rewritten without the Capitalization Rules You Used	Why the Capitalization in the Original Passage Is Important

Figure 4.1.5 Reflection Graphic Organizer

"Before you work on this activity, I'll share my work on my example. I'll write my original passage in the graphic organizer."

They love to dress up on Halloween.

If you use this same example, I suggest writing it in the graphic organizer in Figure 4.1.5 and displaying that information. If you use a different example, please write that one instead.

"I'll now write how that passage would look without the capitalization rules I used."

they love to dress up on halloween.

If you're using this same example, I suggest writing this text in the graphic organizer. If you're using a different example, I recommend writing that text without the capitalization rules used in the passage.

"Next, I'll write why I think the capitalization in the original passage is important. My response is 'The capitalization in the original passage makes the piece clear and easy to understand for the reader. By capitalizing the 'T' in 'they,' I help readers understand that the sentence is supposed to start with the word 'They.' By capitalizing the 'H' in 'Halloween.' I make sure readers know that I'm talking about a specific holiday. If I didn't use these capitalization rules, readers could be confused while reading the passage.'"

If you're using this example, I recommend sharing this explanation or a similar one. If you use a different example, I suggest providing an explanation that corresponds with the example you share.

"You'll now use the graphic organizer to write your original passage, write how it would look without the capitalization rules you used, and share your reflection on why the capitalization in the original passage is important. I'll talk with you about your progress while you work."

I recommend moving around the classroom as students work on this activity and providing them with individualized support.

"Great job on this activity! Let's have two volunteers share. Each volunteer will share their passage, identify the capitalization rules they used in the passage, and explain why the capitalization in the original passage is important. Afterward, everyone will turn in the passage they created in our writing activity and the graphic organizer they completed in this activity."

As students share their work, I suggest pointing out especially strong insights and ideas and providing additional explanation when needed.

5. Exit Question

To conclude this instructional process, students answer an exit question about the importance of capitalization.

"We'll finish our work on capitalization with an exit question about its importance. After you write an answer to the exit question, two volunteers will share their responses, and I'll collect everyone's written answers. The exit question is 'Why is capitalization an important tool for strong writing?'"

I recommend displaying this exit question while reading it aloud. When students share their ideas, I praise the strong points they make.

Differentiation Suggestions

This lesson can be differentiated in numerous ways:

- Students can work with capitalization mentor texts on a range of reading levels so they can read examples that best meet their needs as readers.
- Students can create passages that use additional examples of capitalization rules.
- If there are certain capitalization rules you want students to practice, you can ask them to include those capitalization rules in their passages.

Assessment

I recommend assessing students' knowledge of capitalization and their work in this instruction process in the following ways:

- Students' exit question responses.
  - The answers students provide to the exit questions in this instructional sequence offer key insight into their knowledge of punctuation. When assessing students' work on the day-one exit question, "Why do writers use capitalization in their works?," I recommend evaluating how well students explain that writers use this strategy to help their readers understand their works. When evaluating students' answers to the day-two exit question, "Why is capitalization an important tool for strong writing?," I suggest assessing the clarity and detail students use when explaining that capitalization is important to strong writing because it makes writing clear and helps readers comprehend a piece without being distracted by capitalization mistakes.
- Students' written passages and reflections.
  - I recommend also assessing students' understandings of capitalization by examining the examples they crafted during

the writing activity and the corresponding reflections they created on the graphic organizer depicted in Figure 4.1.5. When evaluating students' work on the writing activity, I look to see if they used capitalization correctly in their passages and if they used at least two of the capitalization rules we discussed. When I assess students' reflections, I evaluate the accuracy, detail, and thoughtfulness in students' statements about why the capitalization in the original passage is important.

Notes

◆ What worked when teaching this lesson?

◆ What might you adapt or change the next time you teach it?

References

Beatty, R. (2015). *Serafina and the black cloak*. Disney Hyperion.
Franklin, M.S. (2015). *Extraordinary*. Sky Pony Press.
Johnson, V. (2018). *The Parker inheritance*. Scholastic.
O'Connor, B. (2016). *Wish*. Farrar Straus Giroux.
Thomas, A. (2023). *Nic Blake and the remarkables: The manifestor prophecy*. Balzer + Bray.
Williams-Garcia, R. (2013). *P.S. Be eleven*. HarperCollins.

LESSON 4.2

Showing Conditions
Modal Auxiliaries

This lesson addresses the grammatical concept of modal auxiliaries, which are words that give information about the possibility, likelihood, or necessity of something happening. The lesson spans two class periods. On the first day, students will learn what modal auxiliaries are, encounter examples of them, examine how writers use them, and think about the impact that modal auxiliaries have on writing. On day two, students will review important modal auxiliary information, apply it to their own writing, and reflect on how modal auxiliaries are important to the effectiveness of their works. At the conclusion of the process, students will think about how this concept can be important to their future writing.

Objectives

- Students will understand the concept of modal auxiliaries.
- Students will understand the impact that modal auxiliaries have on writing.
- Students will be able to apply the concept of modal auxiliaries to their writing and reflect on the importance of doing so.

Time Frame

Two class periods.

DOI: 10.4324/9781003610656-10

Background Knowledge Required

Students need to understand what verbs are and how they're used.

Materials Needed

- Figures 4.2.1–4.2.4. These figures are in the lesson plan, in Appendix B: Reproducible Graphic Organizers, and in electronic format on the book website.
- A board, projector, or piece of chart paper for displaying information.
- Paper for writing activities.

Detailed Plan

Day One
1. Introduction
You'll begin this instructional process by introducing students to the topic of modal auxiliaries, sharing the key questions for the first day of work on the topic, and providing the day's agenda.

"Today, we're going to investigate the grammatical concept of modal auxiliaries. We'll explore these questions:

- What are modal auxiliaries?
- How can modal auxiliaries impact a piece of writing?

Let's check out the agenda for our work today on modal auxiliaries:

- Modal auxiliary mini-lesson
- Mentor text example
- Mentor text discussion and analysis activities
- Exit question"

I recommend displaying the questions and agenda items while sharing them with students.

2. Modal Auxiliary Mini-Lesson
In this mini-lesson on the grammatical concept of modal auxiliaries, you'll introduce students to what modal auxiliaries are, share examples of them, and describe their importance.

"In our mini-lesson, I'm going to share information about modal auxiliaries. This will be the starting point for our work together on this concept. First, let's explore what modal auxiliaries are. Modal auxiliaries are words that give information about the possibility, likelihood, or necessity of something happening. The following words are used as modal auxiliaries: *will, would, shall, should, can, could, may, might, must,* and *ought to.* For example, I might say 'I will go to the game this weekend.' This sentence uses the modal auxiliary 'will,' which shows that I definitely will attend the game. If I said, 'I might go to the game this weekend,' I would be using the modal auxiliary 'might' to show that I am less certain about whether or not I will go to the game. Modal auxiliaries are important to strong writing because writers can use them to show exactly how likely, possible, or necessary something is. They provide clarity and specificity. If we replace one modal auxiliary with another, we change the likelihood, possibility, or necessity expressed in the sentence, which changes the sentence's meaning and tone. Let's look together at an informational chart on modal auxiliaries that contains key information about this topic."

Grammatical Concept	What Are Modal Auxiliaries?	What Words Are Used as Modal Auxiliaries?	What Are Some Ways Modal Auxiliaries Can Look in Writing?	Why Are Modal Auxiliaries Important to Strong Writing?
Modal Auxiliaries	Modal auxiliaries are words that give information about the possibility, likelihood, or necessity of something happening.	The following words are used as modal auxiliaries: *will, would, shall, should, can, could, may, might, must,* and *ought to.*	I **must** leave now. You **should** read this book. I **can** go to the movies.	Modal auxiliaries are important to strong writing because writers can use them to show exactly how likely, possible, or necessary something is.

Figure 4.2.1 Modal Auxiliary Information

I suggest displaying this chart on a projector screen and reading the information to students.

3. Mentor Text Example

You'll now share with students a published sentence that contains a modal auxiliary. This provides students with an example of how modal auxiliaries are used in authentic communication and prepares them for other activities later in the lesson.

"We're going to look together at a published example of how an author uses a modal auxiliary. In the book *Step Up to the Plate, Maria Singh* (Krishnaswami, 2017), author Uma Krishnaswami uses the modal auxiliary 'will' in the sentence 'There will be other girls' teams in the county' (p. 17). In this sentence, a teacher is discussing starting a school softball team. In our next activity, we'll consider the importance of this modal auxiliary to the sentence."

When sharing this modal auxiliary mentor text with students, I recommend displaying it on a slide or piece of chart paper so students can easily see it.

4. Mentor Text Discussion and Analysis Activities

In this part of the lesson, you'll guide students through a discussion of the modal auxiliary mentor text and through related activities constructed to help them understand the impact of the modal auxiliary that the author used on the text. This work is designed to develop students' understandings of the significance of modal auxiliaries.

"Now, we'll think about why the modal auxiliary 'will' is important to the mentor text example from *Step Up to the Plate, Maria Singh*. I'm going to display a chart. On one side of it, you'll see the original mentor text. On the other side, you'll see the sentence from the text, but the modal auxiliary 'will' is replaced with a different modal auxiliary—the word 'might.'"

Original Text	Revised Version with Different Modal Auxiliary
"There will be other girls' teams in the county" (Krishnaswami, 2017, p. 17).	There might be other girls' teams in the county.

Figure 4.2.2 Original Text vs. Revised Version with Different Modal Auxiliary

I like to display these examples on a projector screen or on chart paper while reading them aloud.

"Next, please talk with a partner about these two questions: How is the original sentence with the modal auxiliary 'will' different from the revised version with the modal auxiliary 'might'? and Why is the modal auxiliary 'will' important to the original sentence? After you discuss these questions with a partner, volunteers will share with the class. We'll record volunteers' responses on a graphic organizer that I'll display."

Reflection Question One	Reflection Question Two
How is the original sentence with the modal auxiliary "will" different from the revised version with the modal auxiliary "might"?	Why is the modal auxiliary "will" important to the original sentence?

Figure 4.2.3 Modal Auxiliary Reflection Questions Graphic Organizer

I suggest projecting or recreating this chart and then recording the responses that students share on it.

5. Exit Question
To conclude this class period, students answer an exit question on the impact that modal auxiliaries can have on writing.

"To conclude today's work on modal auxiliaries, you'll answer an exit question on this topic. Please write your answer on a piece of paper. I'll ask for two volunteers to share, and then I'll collect everyone's work. The exit question is 'How can modal auxiliaries impact a piece of writing?'"

I recommend displaying the question while reading it. After collecting students' responses, I suggest examining their answers to evaluate their understanding and using this information to inform your upcoming instruction.

Day Two
1. Introduction
You'll start the second day of work on modal auxiliaries by discussing how the day's work builds on the previous day's activities, sharing the day's focal questions, and presenting the agenda for the class period.

"Great work yesterday on modal auxiliaries! In yesterday's class, we discussed what modal auxiliaries are, looked at examples of them, considered why they are important to strong writing, examined a published example of their use, and reflected on how they can impact a piece of writing. Today, we'll build on that work by continuing to explore modal auxiliaries. First, we'll review key information about this topic. Then, we'll create our own passages that contain modal auxiliaries and reflect on their importance. We'll conclude with an exit question about the importance of modal auxiliaries to our future writing. Our key questions for today are:

- How can we use modal auxiliaries in our writing?
- What impact do the modal auxiliaries we use have on the written works we create?

Here is today's agenda:

- Modal auxiliary review
- Writing activity
- Reflection
- Exit question"

I suggest displaying the key questions and agenda items while sharing them.

2. Modal Auxiliary Review
Here, you'll review key information, ideas, and examples about modal auxiliaries that you shared and discussed the previous day.

"We'll review key points about modal auxiliaries that we discussed yesterday. Let's look together at a chart that reviews what modal auxiliaries are, shows what words are used as modal auxiliaries, explains why they're important to strong writing, and provides a published example of modal auxiliary use."

What Are Modal Auxiliaries?	What Words Are Used as Modal Auxiliaries?	Why Are Modal Auxiliaries Important to Strong Writing?	What Is a Published Example of Modal Auxiliary Use?
Modal auxiliaries are words that give information about the possibility, likelihood, or necessity of something happening.	The following words are used as modal auxiliaries: *will, would, shall, should, can, could, may, might, must,* and *ought to.*	Modal auxiliaries are important to strong writing because writers can use them to show exactly how likely, possible, or necessary something is.	"There **will** be other girls' teams in the county" (Krishnaswami, 2017, p. 17).

Figure 4.2.4 Modal Auxiliary Review Information

I suggest displaying this chart and reading its contents aloud while students follow along. I also like to use this time to discuss any information about modal auxiliaries about which students showed confusion in the previous class.

3. Writing Activity

This activity calls for students to use modal auxiliaries in their writing. They create a written passage containing a modal auxiliary, which provides them with an opportunity to apply their knowledge of this concept.

"Now, we'll use our knowledge of modal auxiliaries in our writing. You'll write a one- or two-sentence passage that uses a modal auxiliary in it. Before you write, I'll share an example I created: 'I <u>can</u> go to the football game this weekend.' I used the modal auxiliary 'can' in my passage to show the possibility, likelihood, or necessity of what I discussed in my sentence, and I underlined that modal auxiliary."

When you teach this lesson, you can use this same example or create a new one to share with your students.

"It's time for you to write! You'll create a passage that shows how likely, possible, or necessary something is, and you'll underline that modal auxiliary like I did in the example. After that, you'll share your work with a partner, and volunteers will share with the class."

As students write, I recommend circulating the classroom to check in on their progress and provide individualized support and encouragement.

"Good job creating those examples. Please share your passage with a partner and identify the modal auxiliary you used."

While students share with partners, I suggest moving around the room, listening to their insights, and providing praise and support.

"Let's take volunteers to share with the class the passage you wrote and point out the modal auxiliary in it."

When volunteers share this work, I recommend praising strong work and providing any explanation or clarification needed.

4. Reflection

In this reflective activity, students revisit the passages they wrote during the writing activity to analyze the importance of the modal auxiliary they used.

"Next, you'll reflect on the importance of the modal auxiliary that you used in your passage. You'll write an answer to this question: 'Why is the modal auxiliary you used in your passage important?'"

I like to post this question while reading it aloud.

"Before you start, I'll share the reflection I wrote about my passage, 'I can go to the football game this weekend.' My answer to the exit question is 'The modal auxiliary can is important because it gives specific information about my ability to go to the football game. It tells the audience that I am able to go to the game. If I used a different modal auxiliary, such as should, I would be giving different information—I would be telling the audience that I should go to the game for some reason, not that I can go. The modal auxiliary can express the information in the sentence accurately and in the way that I intended.'"

If you use this same example with your students, you can share this reflection with them. If you create your own example, you can share a reflection that aligns with that example.

"It's your turn. Revisit the passage you wrote that contains a modal auxiliary and write an answer to the question 'Why is the modal auxiliary you used in your passage important?'"

As students write their reflections, I suggest checking with them to monitor their progress and give feedback.

"Good job writing your reflections. Please share your reflection with a partner and listen when they share theirs."

While students share, I like to move around the classroom, listening to and commenting on their insights.

"I'll now ask for two volunteers to share their reflection question answers with the class. After that, everyone will turn in their reflections and the passages they wrote in the writing activity."

When students share responses, I recommend praising strong statements and building on points that can benefit from additional explanation.

5. Exit Question

To conclude this instructional process, students answer an exit question about the importance of modal auxiliaries to their future writing.

"We'll finish our work on modal auxiliaries with an exit question. After you write your answer, I'll ask for volunteers to share responses. I'll then collect everyone's written answers. The exit question is 'How can modal auxiliaries be important to your future writing?'"

I suggest displaying this question and reading it aloud. When students share responses, I recommend praising strong answers and providing additional elaboration when needed.

Differentiation Suggestions

This lesson can be differentiated in several ways:

- Students can read additional modal auxiliary mentor texts so they can encounter more published examples of this concept.
- Students can explore modal auxiliary mentor texts on a range of reading levels so that they can work with texts that are good fits for them.
- Students can use multiple modal auxiliaries in the passages they create.
- Students can create multiple passages that use modal auxiliaries.

Assessment

I recommend assessing students' knowledge of modal auxiliaries and their work in this instructional process in these ways:

- Students' exit question responses.
    - The exit question responses students create during this lesson sequence provide key insights into their understanding of modal auxiliaries. When assessing students' answers to the day-one exit question, "How can modal auxiliaries impact a piece of writing?," I suggest evaluating how effectively students explain that modal auxiliaries can impact a piece of writing by showing exactly how likely, possible, or necessary something is. When examining students' responses to the day-two exit question,

"How can modal auxiliaries be important to your future writing?," I recommend assessing how well students explain that modal auxiliaries can be important to their future works because they can use modal auxiliaries to express likelihood, possibility, or necessity in their future writing.
- Students' writing activities and corresponding reflections.
  - I also suggest assessing students' knowledge of modal auxiliaries and their importance by reading students' work from the writing activity and the corresponding reflections they wrote. To evaluate students' writing activity work, I look to see if students used a modal auxiliary in their work and if they identified that modal auxiliary. When assessing students' reflections, I consider the accuracy and detail in their statements about why the modal auxiliary in the passage is important.

Notes

- What worked when teaching this lesson?

- What might you adapt or change the next time you teach it?

Reference

Krishnaswami, U. (2017). *Step up to the plate, Maria Singh*. Lee & Low Books.

LESSON 4.3

Elaborating on Information

Prepositional Phrases

Overview

This lesson focuses on prepositional phrases, descriptive phrases that begin with a preposition and end with a noun or pronoun that is the object of that preposition. It spans two class periods. On the first day, students will learn what prepositional phrases are, explore examples of them, examine how writers use them, and consider the impact they have on writing. On the second day, students will review key ideas about prepositional phrases, use them in writing, and reflect on the impact of this concept on the passages they wrote. At the end of the lesson sequence, students answer an exit question about the importance of prepositional phrases to strong writing.

Objectives

- Students will understand the concept of prepositional phrases.
- Students will understand the importance of prepositional phrases to strong writing.
- Students will be able to use prepositional phrases in their writing and reflect on the importance of doing so.

Time Frame

Two class periods.

Background Knowledge Required

No specific background knowledge is required.

Materials Needed

- Figures 4.3.1–4.3.5, which are available in the lesson plan, in Appendix B: Reproducible Graphic Organizers, and in electronic format on the book's website.
- A board, projector, or piece of chart paper to display information.
- Paper for writing activities.

Detailed Plan

Day One
1. Introduction
To introduce this lesson sequence, you'll let students know that they'll be studying prepositional phrases, present the day's key questions, and share the agenda for the day.

"We're going to learn about prepositional phrases, which are phrases that provide detail and description to writing. We'll explore these questions in our work today:

- What are prepositional phrases?
- Why are prepositions phrases important to strong writing?

The agenda for our work today is:

- Prepositional phrase mini-lesson
- Mentor text example
- Mentor text discussion and analysis activities
- Exit question"

I recommend displaying these key questions and agenda items while reading them aloud.

2. Prepositional Phrases Mini-Lesson

You'll teach a mini-lesson on key features of prepositional phrases. In it, you'll introduce students to what prepositional phrases are, provide examples, and discuss the importance of this concept.

"In this mini-lesson, I'll share some key information about prepositional phrases. We'll continue to discuss these ideas as we learn about this topic. Let's first discuss what prepositions are. Prepositions are words that show relationships between information, like where something is, where an action took place, or when it happened. These words begin prepositional phrases. Prepositional phrases are descriptive phrases that begin with a preposition and end with a noun or pronoun called the object of the preposition. For example, in the sentence 'The cat slept on the chair,' the word 'on' is a preposition and 'chair' is the object of a preposition. The prepositional phrase is 'on the chair.' Let's look at some examples of frequently used prepositions."

At	During
Above	In
Across	On
Before	Through
Down	Under

Figure 4.3.1 Some Frequently Used Prepositions

I suggest displaying these preposition examples while reading them to students.

"Now that we've seen examples of frequently used prepositions, let's think some more about prepositional phrases. Another example of a prepositional phrase can be found in the sentence 'The birds flew above the trees.' Here, 'above the trees' is a prepositional phrase—it begins with the preposition 'above' and ends with 'trees,' which is the object of the preposition. Prepositional phrases, like the ones I've shared so far and the others we'll explore, are important to strong writing because of the detail and description they add. This information can give the reader a clear understanding of what's being discussed. Let's look at a chart that highlights key ideas about prepositional phrases."

Grammatical Concept	What Are Prepositional Phrases?	What Are Examples of Prepositional Phrases?	How Can Prepositional Phrases Look in Writing?	Why Are Prepositional Phrases Important to Strong Writing?
Prepositional phrases	Prepositional phrases are descriptive phrases that begin with a preposition and end with a noun or pronoun called the object of the preposition.	On the chair Above the trees Under the desk Across the field	The cat slept **on the chair.** The birds flew **above the trees.** We looked **under the desk.** She kicked the ball **across the field.**	Prepositional phrases are important to strong writing because of the detail and description they add. This information can give the reader a clear understanding of what's being discussed.

Figure 4.3.2 Prepositional Phrase Information

I recommend displaying this chart while talking to students about its contents.

3. Mentor Text Example

Next, you'll share with students an example of a prepositional phrase from a published text. This activity will show students how prepositional phrases are used in authentic situations.

"Now, let's look at a published example of a prepositional phrase. In the book *Front Desk* (2018), author Kelly Yang uses a prepositional phrase in the sentence 'I counted the keys in my hand' (p. 29). In this sentence, the prepositional phrase 'in my hand' adds description. In our next activity, we'll explore the importance of this prepositional phrase to the passage."

I suggest displaying this prepositional phrase mentor text so that students can follow along while you read it.

4. Mentor Text Discussion and Analysis Activities

In this part of the lesson, you'll guide students through a discussion of the prepositional phrase mentor text and through related activities constructed to help them understand the importance of the prepositional phrase in that text. This work can develop students' awareness of the significance of prepositional phrases.

"Now, we'll think about why the prepositional phrase 'in my hand' is important to the mentor text example we explored from *Front Desk*. Let's look at the original text compared with a revised version that doesn't contain the prepositional phrase."

Original Text	Revised Version with Prepositional Phrase Removed
"I counted the keys in my hand" (Yang, 2018, p. 29).	I counted the keys.

Figure 4.3.3 Original Text vs. Revised Version with Prepositional Phrase Removed

I like to display these examples so that students can follow along while I share them.

"Next, you'll talk with a partner about two reflection questions: How is the sentence different without the prepositional phrase 'in my hand'? and Why do you think the author used this prepositional phrase? After you discuss these questions with your partners, I'll ask for volunteers to share with the class. We'll record responses on a graphic organizer."

Reflection Question One	Reflection Question Two
How is the sentence different without the prepositional phrase "in my hand"?	Why do you think the author used this prepositional phrase?

Figure 4.3.4 Prepositional Phrase Reflection Questions Graphic Organizer

I recommend displaying this chart or recreating it so that it can be easily seen. When students share their ideas, I suggest recording highlights on the chart.

5. Exit Question

To conclude this class period, students answer an exit question related to what they learned that day about prepositional phrases.

"For today's final activity on prepositional phrases, you'll answer an exit question. Please write your answer on a piece of paper. After you write, I'll ask two volunteers to share their responses, and I'll collect everyone's work. The exit question is 'Why would writers use prepositional phrases in their work?'"

I recommend displaying this question while you read it and students write their answers. After collecting students' work, I suggest examining their responses to evaluate their understanding and using this information to inform your upcoming instruction.

Day Two
1. Introduction

To open the second day of work on prepositional phrases, you'll share with students how the work they'll do that day builds on the previous lesson, provide the day's focal questions, and discuss the class period's agenda.

"Wonderful job yesterday working on prepositional phrases! We learned key information about prepositional phrases, examined a published example from *Front Desk* by Kelly Yang (2018), reflected on the importance of that prepositional phrase, and answered an exit question about why writers use prepositional phrases. We'll build on that work in today's class as we explore prepositional phrases further. We'll first review important information about prepositional phrases. Then, we'll use prepositional phrases in our writing and consider their significance. We'll close with an exit question about why prepositional phrases are important tools for strong writing. Today's key questions are:

- How can we use prepositional phrases in our writing?
- How do prepositional phrases enhance our writing?

Our agenda for today is:

- Prepositional phrase review
- Writing activity
- Reflection
- Exit question"

I suggest displaying the questions and agenda items while sharing them with students.

2. Prepositional Phrase Review

In this section of the lesson, you'll review key ideas, examples, and information about prepositional phrases you discussed with students the previous day.

"We'll review some key information about prepositional phrases that we discussed yesterday. Let's look together at a chart that reviews what prepositional phrases are, shares examples of them, discusses why they're important to strong writing, and includes a published mentor text containing a prepositional phrase."

What Are Prepositional Phrases?	What Are Some Examples of Prepositional Phrases?	Why Are Prepositional Phrases Important to Strong Writing?	What Is a Published Example of Prepositional Phrase Use?
Prepositional phrases are descriptive phrases that begin with a preposition and end with a noun or pronoun called the object of the preposition.	On the chair Above the trees Under the desk Across the field	Prepositional phrases are important to strong writing because of the detail and description they add. This information can give the reader a clear understanding of what's being discussed.	"I counted the keys **in my hand**" (Yang, 2018, p. 29).

Figure 4.3.5 Prepositional Phrase Review Information

I suggest displaying this chart and reading its contents aloud while students follow along. I also like to use this time to discuss anything about prepositional phrases that may have confused students in the previous day's class.

3. Writing Activity

Next, students apply prepositional phrases to their writing by creating a passage that uses a prepositional phrase to provide detail and description.

"Now, we'll apply our knowledge of our prepositional phrases to our own writing! You'll create a one- or two-sentence passage on the topic of your choice that uses a prepositional phrase to provide detail and description. Here is an example of a passage with a prepositional phrase that I created:

'The deer ran <u>through the forest</u>.' I used the prepositional phrase 'through the forest' to provide detail and description about where the deer ran. I underlined it in the passage."

You can use this prepositional phrase example or create one of your own to share with students.

"It's time now for you to create a passage that uses a prepositional phrase to add detail and description like I did in the example. Then, you'll share your work with a partner; volunteers will share with the class."

As students create these examples, I recommend circulating the classroom to monitor their progress, supporting their work, and praising strong writing.

"Let's take two volunteers to share your passage with the class and identify the prepositional phrase in it."

When students share their work with the class, I suggest praising strong responses and providing any needed clarification.

4. Reflection

In this reflective activity, students return to the passage they wrote and analyze the importance of the prepositional phrase they used.

"For our next activity, you'll reflect on the importance of the prepositional phrase to the passage you just created. You'll write an answer to the question 'Why is the prepositional phrase you used important to your passage?'"

"Before you reflect, I'll share what I wrote about my passage 'The deer ran through the forest.' My answer to the reflection question is 'The prepositional phrase through the forest is important to my passage because it provides detail and description about where the deer ran. This prepositional phrase elaborates on the statement that the deer ran by explaining where it ran. By providing this detail, description, and elaboration, the prepositional phrase gives the reader a clear understanding of what's happening in the sentence.'"

If you use this same passage with your students, you can share this reflection. If you write your own passage, you can construct a reflection aligned with that passage.

"Please revisit the passage you created and write an answer to the question 'Why is the prepositional phrase you used important to your passage?'"

While students write their reflections, I suggest moving around the classroom to check on their progress in answering the question and to provide them with needed support.

"Good job writing those reflections. Now, share your reflection with a partner and listen while they share theirs."

When students share with partners, I recommend listening to and commenting on their insights.

"We'll take two volunteers to share their reflections with the class. After that, I'll ask everyone to turn in these reflections and the passages you wrote in the writing activity."

As students share answers, I like to praise strong insights and build on statements that can be enhanced further.

5. Exit Question

At the end of this instructional process, students answer an exit question about the importance of prepositional phrases to strong writing.

"We'll wrap up our work on prepositional phrases with an exit question on this topic. You'll write an answer to the exit question, and then I'll ask for volunteers to share. Then, I'll collect all of the written answers. The exit question is 'Why are prepositional phrases important tools for strong writing?'"

I recommend displaying this question while reading it aloud. When volunteers share their work, I suggest complimenting *especially strong points and elaborating on statements that can benefit from additional information.*

Differentiation Suggestions

This lesson can be differentiated in numerous ways:

- Students can engage with additional prepositional phrase mentor texts so they can see more examples of prepositional phrases in published writing.
- Students work with prepositional phrase mentor texts on a range of reading levels so they can read texts that best fit them.
- Students can use multiple prepositional phrases in the passages they write.
- Students can create multiple passages that include prepositional phrases.

Assessment

I suggest assessing students' knowledge of prepositional phrases and their work in this instructional process in two ways:

- Students' exit question responses.
  - The two exit question responses students write during this instructional process can be very useful when assessing their knowledge of prepositional phrases. When evaluating students' responses to the day-one exit question, "Why would writers use prepositional phrases in their work?," I recommend assessing how well students explain that writers use prepositional phrases to add detail and description to their work. When evaluating students'

answers to the day-two exit question, "Why are prepositional phrases important tools for strong writing?," I suggest assessing if students are able to explain that prepositional phrases are important because they provide detail and description, which can give the reader a clear understanding of what's being discussed.
- Students' writing activities and corresponding reflections.
  - Students' work on the writing activity and the corresponding reflections they wrote are also excellent ways to assess their knowledge of prepositional phrases. When evaluating students' work on the writing activity, I assess if students used a prepositional phrase in their passage, if they identified the prepositional phrase, and if that prepositional phrase makes sense for the passage. When assessing students' reflections, I evaluate the clarity, insight, and detail present in students' comments about the importance of the prepositional phrase they used in the passage they created.

Notes

- What worked when teaching this lesson?

- What might you adapt or change the next time you teach it?

Reference

Yang, K. (2018). *Front desk*. Scholastic.

LESSON 4.4

Providing Detail

Relative Clauses

Overview

This lesson addresses relative clauses, grammatical tools that provide detail and description about nouns and pronouns and begin with relative pronouns or relative adverbs. It spans two class periods. On day one, students will learn what relative clauses are, see examples of them, explore how writers use them, and think about the impact they have on writing. On day two, students will review key information about relative clauses, apply them to their writing, and reflect on the significance of this concept to their written works. The instructional process concludes with students answering an exit question on the importance of relative clauses to strong writing.

Objectives

- Students will understand the concept of relative clauses.
- Students will understand the importance of relative clauses to strong writing.
- Students will be able to use relative clauses in their writing and reflect on the importance of the concept to their works.

Time Frame

Two class periods.

Background Knowledge Required

Students will need to know what nouns and pronouns are in order to understand what relative clauses describe.

Materials Needed

- Figures 4.4.1–4.4.5. These figures are available in the lesson plan, in Appendix B: Reproducible Graphic Organizers, and on the book's website.
- A board, projector, or piece of chart paper to display information.
- Paper for use in writing activities.

Detailed Plan

Day One
1. Introduction
You'll introduce this lesson sequence by informing students that they'll be studying prepositional phrases, sharing the key questions for the day, and presenting the day's agenda.

"We're going to explore the concept of relative clauses, which are grammatical tools that provide detail and description about nouns or pronouns and begin with relative pronouns or relative adverbs. Here are key questions we'll keep in mind today:

- What are relative clauses?
- Why are relative clauses important to strong writing?

Our agenda for today's work is:

- Relative clause mini-lesson
- Mentor text example
- Mentor text discussion and analysis activities
- Exit question"

I suggest displaying these questions and agenda items while reading them aloud.

2. Relative Clause Mini-Lesson
You'll now teach a mini-lesson on relative clauses. In this mini-lesson, you'll share information about what relative clauses are, provide examples, and describe the importance of this concept.

"In our mini-lesson on relative clauses, we'll consider key information on this concept. As we continue to learn about relative clauses, we'll keep exploring these ideas. First, let's talk about what relative clauses are. Relative clauses are grammatical tools that provide detail and description about nouns or pronouns and begin with relative pronouns or relative adverbs. Let's explore what relative pronouns and relative adverbs are."

Relative Pronouns	Relative Adverbs
Who, Whose, Whom, Which, That	Where, When, Why

Figure 4.4.1 Relative Pronouns and Relative Adverbs

I suggest displaying this chart while sharing its information with students.

"These words can begin relative clauses by introducing the detail and description that relative clauses provide. For example, the relative pronoun 'who' could begin the relative clause 'who loves the snow.' We could use that relative clause in a sentence by writing 'Liz, who loves the snow, is sledding.' The relative adverb 'where' could begin the relative clause 'where the Boston Red Sox play.' If we used that relative clause in a sentence, we could say 'We visited Fenway Park, where the Boston Red Sox play.' These relative clauses provide detail and description about the nouns they're modifying. Let's look at a chart that shares important information about relative clauses."

Grammatical Concept	What Are Relative Clauses?	What Are Examples of Relative Clauses?	How Can Relative Clauses Look in Writing?	Why Are Relative Clauses Important to Strong Writing?
Relative clauses	Relative clauses are grammatical tools that provide detail and description about nouns or pronouns and begin with relative pronouns or relative adverbs.	who loves the snow where the Boston Red Sox play which is her favorite sport	Liz, **who loves the snow**, is sledding. We visited Fenway Park, **where the Boston Red Sox play**. Tomorrow, Kim will play basketball, **which is her favorite sport**.	Relative clauses are important to strong writing because the detail and description they provide can enhance the reader's understanding of the noun or pronoun being discussed.

Figure 4.4.2 Relative Clause Information

I recommend displaying this chart and discussing its contents with students.

3. Mentor Text Example

In this part of the lesson, you'll share with students a published passage that contains a relative clause. This shows students an authentic example of relative clause use.

"Let's check out an example of how a published author uses a relative clause. In the book *Bayou Magic* (2016), author Jewell Parker Rhodes uses the relative clause 'which is creased from the ridges on the seat' to provide detail and description in the sentence 'I rub my cheek, which is creased from the ridges on the seat' (p. 12). Next, we'll think in-depth about the importance of this relative clause to the sentence."

I suggest displaying this relative clause mentor text and asking students to follow along as you read it aloud.

4. Mentor Text Discussion and Analysis Activities

Here, you'll help students think about and analyze the importance of the relative clause to the mentor text they encountered in the previous step of the instructional process. Doing so can develop students' understandings of the importance of relative clauses.

"Now that we've seen a published example of a relative clause, we're going to think about why that relative clause is important to the published work we read. Let's look at the mentor text from *Bayou Magic* compared with a revised version of the sentence that doesn't contain the relative clause."

Original Text	Revised Version with Relative Clause Removed
"I rub my cheek, which is creased from the ridges on the seat" (Rhodes, 2016, p. 12).	I rub my cheek.

Figure 4.4.3 Original Text vs. Revised Version with Relative Clause Removed

I suggest displaying these examples while sharing them with students.

"Please talk with a partner about two reflection questions: How is the sentence different without the relative clause 'which is created from the ridges on the seat'? and Why do you think the author used this relative clause? After you and your partner discuss these questions, volunteers will share with the class, and I'll record answers on a graphic organizer."

Reflection Question One	Reflection Question Two
How is the sentence different without the relative clause "which is created from the ridges on the seat"?	Why do you think the author used this relative clause?

Figure 4.4.4 Relative Clause Reflection Question Graphic Organizer

I recommend displaying this chart and recording highlights from students' responses on it.

5. Exit Question
This class period concludes with students answering an exit question about relative clauses.

"Our final relative clause activity for today is an exit question. Please write your answer to the exit question on a piece of paper. After you do this, I'll ask for volunteers to share, and I'll collect everyone's written answers. The exit question is 'Why would writers use relative clauses in their work?'"

I suggest displaying this question and reading it as students write their answers. After I collect students' written responses, I evaluate their answers to assess their understandings of relative clauses. I use this information to shape my future instruction.

Day Two
1. Introduction
You'll begin the second day of work on relative clauses by explaining how that day's work will build on what they did during the first day, sharing the day's key questions, and presenting the agenda for the class period.

"Great work yesterday on relative clauses! You learned key information about relative clauses, examined a relative clause mentor text from the book *Bayou Magic* by Jewell Parker Rhodes (2016), thought about the importance of the relative clause the author used, and answered an exit question about why writers would use relative clauses in their work. Today, we'll build on that work and think further about relative clauses. We'll start by reviewing important information about relative clauses. Then, we'll apply our knowledge of relative clauses and reflect on the significance of doing so. To conclude our work, we'll answer an exit question about why relative clauses are important tools for strong writing. Our key questions for today are:

- How can we use relative clauses in our writing?
- How can using relative clauses enhance our writing?

Today's agenda is:

- Relative clause review
- Writing activity
- Reflection
- Exit question"

I recommend displaying these questions and agenda items while reading them to students.

2. Relative Clause Review
In this part of the lesson, you'll review essential information, ideas, and examples related to relative clauses that you discussed previously.

"Let's review key points about relative clauses discussed in yesterday's class. We'll look at a chart that reviews what relative clauses are, provides examples of them, describes why they're important to strong writing, and shares a mentor text containing a relative clause."

What Are Relative Clauses?	What Are Some Examples of Relative Clauses?	Why Are Relative Clauses Important to Strong Writing?	What Is a Published Example of Relative Clause Use?
Relative clauses are grammatical tools that provide detail and description about nouns or pronouns and begin with relative pronouns or relative adverbs.	who loves the snow where the Boston Red Sox play which is her favorite sport	Relative clauses are important to strong writing because the detail and description they provide can enhance the reader's understanding of the noun or pronoun being discussed.	"I rub my cheek, **which is creased from the ridges on the seat**" (Rhodes, 2016, p. 12).

Figure 4.4.5 Relative Clause Review Information

I recommend displaying this information and reading it aloud while students follow along. If students showed any confusion about relative clauses in the previous class, I suggest using this time to provide any needed clarification.

3. Writing Activity

In this activity, students apply relative clauses to their writing by creating a passage that contains a relative clause to provide detail and description about a noun or pronoun.

"We'll now put our knowledge of relative clauses into action by using them in our writing! You'll write a one- to two-sentence passage that contains a relative clause. You'll use that relative clause to provide detail and description about a noun or pronoun. Before you write, I'll share an example I created. I wrote the passage 'Mrs. Smith, who is very friendly, greeted us at the door.' I used the relative clause 'who is very friendly' to provide detail and description about the noun Mrs. Smith."

You can use this same relative clause example in this lesson, or you can create your own to share with students.

"Now, it's your turn! You'll create a passage that uses a relative clause to provide detail and description about a noun or pronoun like I did in my example. You'll share what you wrote with a partner. Then, volunteers will share with the class."

When students work on their examples, I like to move around the classroom to monitor their work, provide support, and recognize strong writing.

"I'll now ask for two volunteers to share your passage with the class and identify the relative clause you used."

As volunteers share their examples, I recommend praising strong work and sharing extra explanations when needed.

4. Reflection

Next, students return to the passage they created and analyze the importance of the relative clause they used.

"Now that you've written a passage containing a relative clause, you'll reflect on the importance of that relative clause to the passage you created. You'll write an answer to the question 'Why is the relative clause you used important to your passage?'"

"I'll provide an example by sharing what I wrote about my passage 'Mrs. Smith, who is very friendly, greeted us at the door.' My answer to the reflection question is 'The relative clause who is very friendly is important to this passage because of the information it provides about Mrs. Smith. It gives detail and description about Mrs. Smith that helps the reader understand key information about Mrs. Smith. Without this relative clause, readers wouldn't know from this sentence that Mrs. Smith is very friendly.'"

You can use this reflection with your students if you use the same passage I provided. If you create your own passage, you can share a reflection that corresponds with that passage.

"It's your turn! Reread your passage and then write an answer to the reflection question 'Why is the relative clause you used important to your passage?'"

As students write answers to the reflection question, I like to circulate the classroom, providing needed support and praising strong work.

"Good job! Please now share your reflection with a partner; they'll then share theirs with you."

While students share with partners, I suggest listening to their statements and commenting on the insights they share.

"Let's have two volunteers share their reflections with the class. Then, everyone will turn in their reflections and their passages from the writing activity."

When volunteer share their reflections, I recommend noting strong statements and providing additional explanation and clarification if needed.

5. Exit Question

This instructional process concludes with students answering an exit question about the importance of relative clauses to strong writing.

"For our activity on relative clauses, you'll write an answer to an exit question on this topic, and then I'll ask for two volunteers to share their responses with the class. Then, I'll collect everyone's written answers. The exit question is 'Why are relative clauses important tools for strong writing?'"

I suggest displaying this question while reading it aloud. When volunteers share responses, I recommend complimenting strong insights and clarifying responses if needed.

Differentiation Suggestions

There are many ways this lesson can be differentiated:

- Students can work with additional relative clause mentor texts, showing them more published examples of relative clauses.
- Students can read relative clause mentor texts on a range of reading levels to help them find mentor texts that work best for them.
- Students can use multiple relative clauses in the passages they write.
- Students can compose multiple passages containing relative clauses.

Assessment

I suggest assessing students' knowledge of relative clauses and their work in this lesson sequence in two ways:

- Students' exit question responses.
  - The answers that students submit to the two exit questions can show their understandings of relative clauses and the importance of this concept to strong writing. When evaluating students' responses to the day-one exit question, "Why would writers use relative clauses in their work?," I suggest assessing how effectively students explain that writers use relative clauses to provide detail and description about nouns or pronouns in their writing. When assessing students' answers to the day-two exit question, "Why are relative clauses important tools for strong writing?," I recommend evaluating how well students explain that relative clauses are important to strong writing because the detail and description they provide can enhance the reader's understanding of the noun or pronoun being discussed.

- Students' written passages and corresponding reflections.
  - The written passages students create in the writing activity and the corresponding reflections they compose are also excellent ways to assess students' knowledge of relative clauses. When evaluating students' written passages, I assess if students used a relative clause in their passage, if they identified the relative clause, if the relative clause provides detail and description about a noun or pronoun, and if the relative clause makes sense for the piece. When evaluating students' work on their reflections, I consider the levels of insight and detail present in students' statements about the importance of the relative they used to the passage they created.

Notes

- What worked when teaching this lesson?

- What might you adapt or change the next time you teach it?

Reference

Rhodes, J.P. (2016). *Bayou magic*. Little, Brown Books for Young Readers.

LESSON 4.5

Clear and Powerful Language

Strong Verbs and Specific Nouns

Overview

This lesson addresses the concepts of strong verbs and specific nouns, grammatical tools that authors use to communicate information clearly. The lesson spans two class periods. On day one, students will learn what strong verbs and specific nouns are, see examples of their use, explore published examples of these concepts, and consider their impacts. On day two, students will review strong verbs and specific nouns, apply these concepts in their writing, and reflect on the significance of using them. At the conclusion of the instructional process, students will consider how strong verbs and specific nouns can be important tools to use in their future writing.

Objectives

- Students will understand the concepts of strong verbs and specific nouns.
- Students will understand the importance of strong verbs and specific nouns to strong writing.
- Students will be able to use strong verbs and specific nouns in their writing and reflect on the importance of doing so.

DOI: 10.4324/9781003610656-13

Time Frame

Two class periods.

Background Knowledge Required

Students will need to be familiar with the concepts of verbs and nouns.

Materials Needed

- Figures 4.5.1–4.5.4, available in the lesson plan, in Appendix B: Reproducible Graphic Organizers, and on the book's website.
- A board, projector, or piece of chart paper to display information.
- Paper for writing activities.

Detailed Plan

Day One
1. Introduction
You'll begin this instructional process by introducing students to the concepts of strong verbs and specific nouns, sharing the key questions they'll explore on the first day working on this topic, and presenting the day's agenda.

"Today, we're going to begin examining the concepts of strong verbs and specific nouns. We'll think about these questions:

- What are strong verbs and specific nouns?
- Why are strong verbs and specific nouns important to strong writing?

Here's the agenda for our work today:

- Strong verb and specific noun mini-lesson
- Mentor text examples
- Mentor text discussion and analysis activities
- Exit question"

I suggest displaying these questions and agenda items while sharing them with students.

2. Strong Verb and Specific Noun Mini-Lesson

Next, you'll teach a mini-lesson on strong verbs and specific nouns. In it, you'll describe what these concepts are, provide examples of them, and discuss their importance to strong writing.

"In this mini-lesson, we'll think about key information about strong verbs and specific nouns. We'll continue to consider these ideas as we keep discussing these concepts. We'll begin by discussing what these concepts are. Strong verbs are verbs that clearly show exactly how an action was performed. For example, in the sentence 'I sprinted down the street,' the verb 'sprinted' is a strong verb because it shows exactly how I performed the action. A weaker verb that could be used in this situation could be 'went.' If I wrote 'I went down the street,' I wouldn't show exactly how I performed the action."

"Similarly, specific nouns are nouns that clearly indicate the person, place, thing, or idea being described. In the sentence 'We smelled pizza as we entered the restaurant,' both 'pizza' and 'restaurant' are specific nouns. A version of this sentence with more general nouns could be 'We smelled food as we entered the building.' 'Pizza' and 'restaurant' are more specific than 'food' and 'building.' These specific nouns show exactly what I'm referring to. Strong verbs and specific nouns are important to strong writing because they communicate information clearly and help the reader understand what the writer is discussing. Let's look together at a chart that contains key information about strong verbs and specific nouns."

Grammatical Concepts	What Are Strong Verbs and Specific Nouns?	What Are Examples of Strong Verbs and Specific Nouns?	How Can Strong Verbs and Specific Nouns Look in Writing?	Why Are Strong Verbs and Specific Nouns Important to Strong Writing?
Strong verbs and specific nouns	**Strong verbs** are verbs that clearly show exactly how an action was performed. **Specific nouns** are nouns that clearly indicate the person, place, thing, or idea being described.	**Strong verb examples:** Sprinted Whispered **Specific noun examples:** Pizza Restaurant	**Strong verb examples in writing:** I **sprinted** down the street. He **whispered** the information. **Specific noun examples in writing:** We smelled **pizza** as we entered the **restaurant**.	Strong verbs and specific nouns are important to strong writing because they communicate information clearly and help the reader understand what the writer is discussing.

Figure 4.5.1 Strong Verb and Specific Noun Information

I suggest displaying this chart and reading its contents aloud for students.

3. Mentor Text Examples

Here, you'll share with students published examples of strong verbs and specific nouns. By encountering these examples, students can see authentic examples of these grammatical concepts in action.

"We're going to look at published examples of strong verbs and specific nouns. First, let's check out a published strong verb example. In the book *Me, Frida, and the Secret of the Peacock Ring* (2019), author Angela Cervantes uses the strong verb 'glanced' in the sentence 'Paloma glanced at the black cat and monkey in the painting' (p. 10). This strong verb shows the reader exactly how the character named Paloma performed this action."

"Now, we'll look at a published specific noun example. In the book *The Thing About Luck* (2014), author Cynthia Kadohata uses the specific noun 'mosquito' in the sentence 'This infected mosquito might bite you' (p. 2). By using this specific noun, Kadohata ensures that readers understand exactly what is being discussed."

I recommend displaying these mentor text examples and reading them aloud as students follow along.

4. Mentor Text Discussion and Analysis Activities

You'll now lead students through activities designed to help them think about the importance of the strong verb and specific noun to the mentor texts they previously examined.

"We'll return to the published mentor texts we just saw and analyze the importance of the strong verb to its mentor text and the importance of the specific noun to its mentor text. First, let's think about the strong verb mentor text. I'll display a chart that lists the following information: the original strong verb mentor text, a revised version of the mentor text with the strong verb replaced by a weaker one, and a reflection question about the importance of the strong verb to the original text. I'll read the two passages, and you'll discuss the reflection question with a partner. After you and your partner discuss the reflection question, volunteers will share with the class. I'll then write responses on the graphic organizer."

I recommend reading the original mentor text and the revised version while students follow along. After students discuss the reflection question with a partner, I recommend asking volunteers to share responses and recording response highlights on the graphic organizer.

"Great job on your strong verb analysis! Now, we'll do a similar activity with our specific noun mentor text. I'll display a graphic organizer that contains the original specific noun mentor text, a revised version with the

Clear and Powerful Language ◆ 119

Original Text	Revised Version with Strong Verb Replaced by a Weaker Verb	Reflection Question
"Paloma **glanced** at the black cat and monkey in the painting" (Cervantes, 2019, p. 10).	Paloma **looked** at the black cat and monkey in the painting.	**Question:** Why do you think the strong verb "glanced" is important to the original text? **Our responses:**

Figure 4.5.2 Strong Verb Mentor Text Analysis Graphic Organizer

specific noun replaced by a more general one, and a reflection question about the importance of the specific noun to the original text. I'll read the passages, you'll discuss the reflection question with a partner, and volunteers will share answers with the class. I'll write responses on the graphic organizer."

Original Text	**Revised Version with Specific Noun Replaced by a More General Noun**	**Reflection Question**
"This infected **mosquito** might bite you" (Kadohata, 2014, p. 2).	This infected **insect** might bite you.	**Question:** Why do you think the specific noun "mosquito" is important to the original text? **Our responses:**

Figure 4.5.3 Specific Noun Mentor Text Analysis Graphic Organizer

I suggest reading the original mentor text, the revised version, and the reflection question before asking students to discuss that question with a partner. After the partner discussion, I recommend asking for volunteers to share responses and recording those answers on the graphic organizer.

5. Exit Question

This class period concludes with students answering an exit question on strong verbs and specific nouns.

"Our last activity for today on strong verbs and specific nouns is an exit question. You'll write an answer to an exit question, I'll ask for two volunteers to share with the class, and then I'll collect everyone's responses. The exit question is 'Why would writers use strong verbs and specific nouns in their works?'"

I suggest displaying this question while students write their answers. I like to review students' responses to assess their understanding of strong verbs and specific nouns. This information can then influence future instruction.

Day Two
1. Introduction

To begin the second day of work on strong verbs and specific nouns, you'll discuss how the day's work will build on the previous one, share the key questions for the day, and present the agenda.

"Excellent job yesterday working on strong verbs and specific nouns! You learned key information about these concepts, saw published examples of them, thought about the importance of these concepts to the published texts in which they were used, and answered an exit question about why writers would use these concepts. Today, we'll think even further about strong verbs and specific nouns. We'll review important ideas about them, write passages that use these concepts, reflect on the importance of using them in our work, and answer an exit question about how strong verbs and specific nouns can be important tools to use in your future writing. Today's key questions are:

- How can we use strong verbs and specific nouns in our writing?
- How does using strong verbs and specific nouns make our writing as strong as possible?

Our agenda for today is:

- Strong verb and specific noun review
- Writing activity

- Reflection
- Exit question"

I suggest displaying the questions and agenda while reading them aloud.

2. Strong Verb and Specific Noun Review

You'll review important information about strong verbs and specific nouns discussed in the previous class.

"Let's review key ideas about strong verbs and specific nouns discussed yesterday by looking at a review chart. The chart reviews what strong verbs and specific nouns are, provides examples of them, discusses their importance to strong writing, and includes published examples of them."

What Are Strong Verbs and Specific Nouns?	What Are Examples of Strong Verbs and Specific Nouns?	Why Are Strong Verbs and Specific Nouns Important to Strong Writing?	What Are Published Examples of Strong Verbs and Specific Nouns?
Strong verbs are verbs that clearly show exactly how an action was performed. **Specific nouns** are nouns that clearly indicate the person, place, thing, or idea being described.	**Strong verb examples:** Sprinted Whispered **Specific noun examples:** Pizza Restaurant	Strong verbs and specific nouns are important to strong writing because they communicate information clearly and help the reader understand what the writer is discussing.	**Published strong verb example:** "Paloma **glanced** at the black cat and monkey in the painting" (Cervantes, 2019, p. 10). **Published specific noun example:** "This infected **mosquito** might bite you" (Kadohata, 2014, p. 2).

Figure 4.5.4 Strong Verb and Specific Noun Review Information

I suggest displaying this chart and reading it aloud as students follow along. This is also a great time to address any confusion about strong verbs and specific nouns that students expressed in the previous class.

3. Writing Activity

Here, students apply strong verbs and specific nouns to their writing: each student creates a sentence that contains a strong verb and a specific noun.

"Let's now apply our knowledge of strong verbs and specific nouns to our writing! You'll write a sentence that uses a strong verb and a specific noun. Doing this will help you clearly express information in your passage and help the reader understand what you're discussing. Before you create your example, I'll share one I created. I wrote 'At the zoo, we <u>strolled</u> past the <u>lions</u>.' I used the strong verb 'strolled' and the specific noun 'lions' to make my sentence as clear as possible."

You can use this same example of strong verb and specific noun use, or you can create your own to share with students.

"Now, you'll create a sentence that uses a strong verb and a specific noun like I did in my example. Once you do so, share your example with a partner: read them your sentence and tell them the strong verb and specific noun you used. After that, volunteers will share with the class."

While students share their work with partners, I circulate the classroom, providing support and praise.

"Good job sharing your examples with your partners. Now, let's have two volunteers share their sentences and identify the strong verbs and specific nouns in the sentence."

When volunteers share their sentences and identify their strong verbs and specific nouns, I suggest praising strong examples and providing clarification and support when needed.

4. Reflection

Students now return to their written passages and reflect on the importance of the strong verbs and specific nouns they used.

"For our next activity, you'll revisit the sentence you just wrote and answer two reflection questions about that sentence: 'Why is the strong verb you used important to your sentence?' and 'Why is the specific noun you used important to your sentence?'"

"I'll share my answers to these questions based on my sentence 'At the zoo, we strolled past the lions.' In response to the reflection question 'Why is the strong verb you used important to your sentence?,' I wrote 'The strong verb strolled is important because it shows the exact way we went past the lions and helps the reader picture the action in the way it happened. If I used a weaker verb like "went," "moved," or "walked," readers wouldn't be able to picture the action in the exact way it took place.' For the reflection question 'Why is the specific noun you used important to your sentence?,' I wrote 'The specific noun lions is important to the sentence because it tells the reader exactly what I'm discussing. If I used a more general noun like animals, readers wouldn't have a clear understanding of what we strolled past.'"

If you use these examples, you can share these reflections with students. If you create different examples, you can *share reflections aligned with those examples.*

"You'll now reread your written passages and use them to write answers to the two reflection questions: 'Why is the strong verb you used important to your sentence?' and 'Why is the specific noun you used important to your sentence?' Once you've written those responses, share them with a partner. After you do so, volunteers will share with the class."

As students share with partners, I suggest moving around the room and commenting on their insights.

"Let's now take two volunteers to share their answers to the reflection questions with the class."

When volunteers share their responses, I like to compliment especially strong insights and elaborate on any statements that can benefit from further explanation.

5. Exit Question

This instructional process concludes with students answering an exit question about the importance of strong verbs and specific nouns to their future writing.

"We'll conclude our work on strong verbs and specific nouns with an exit question. You'll write your answer to the question, volunteers will share responses, and I'll collect everyone's work. The exit question is 'How can strong verbs and specific nouns be important tools to use in your future writing?'"

I recommend displaying this question while reading it aloud. As students share responses, I praise strong points and provide any needed clarification and explanation.

Differentiation Suggestions

This lesson can be differentiated in numerous ways:

- Students can examine additional mentor texts featuring strong verbs and specific nouns to show them more ways these concepts can look in published writing.
- Students can explore strong verb and specific noun mentor texts on a range of reading levels so they can work with texts that are good fits for them.
- Students can use multiple strong verbs and specific nouns in the passages they write.
- Students can create additional passages that use strong verbs and specific nouns.

Assessment

I recommend assessing students' work on strong verbs and specific nouns in this lesson sequence in two ways:

- ◆ Students' exit question responses.
  - The two exit question responses students write in this lesson sequence are excellent ways to assess their understandings of strong verbs and specific nouns. When evaluating students' answers to the day-one exit question, "Why would writers use strong verbs and specific nouns in their works?," I assess how well students explain that writers use these concepts to help the reader understand what is being discussed in the text. To assess students' responses to the day-two exit question, "How can strong verbs and specific nouns be important tools to use in your future writing?," I evaluate how effectively students explain that these concepts can help them communicate information clearly in their future writing.
- ◆ Students' written passages and accompanying reflections.
  - The written passages that students created using strong verbs and specific nouns and the corresponding reflections are great for assessing students' knowledge of these concepts. When evaluating students' written passages, I assess if they used strong verbs and specific nouns in their works and if those examples make sense for the passage they wrote. To assess their reflections, I consider the insight and detail present in their discussions of why the strong verb and specific noun each student used are important to the passage.

Notes

- ◆ What worked when teaching this lesson?

♦ What might you adapt or change the next time you teach it?

References

Cervantes, A. (2019). *Me, Frida, and the secret of the peacock ring*. Scholastic.

Kadohata, C. (2014). *The thing about luck*. Atheneum Books For Young Readers.

SECTION THREE

Lesson Plans Recommended for the Fifth-Grade Classroom

LESSON 5.1
Linking and Connecting Conjunctions

Overview

This lesson addresses the grammatical concept of conjunctions, tools that authors use to connect statements. The two-day lesson sequence focuses on three conjunction types: coordinating, correlative, and subordinating. On day one, students will learn what these conjunction types are, examine examples of them, see how writers use them, and consider their impact on writing. On day two, students will review key information about coordinating, correlative, and subordinating conjunctions, create examples of each, and reflect on the benefits of using each one. At the conclusion of the instructional process, students reflect on how the use of conjunctions can be important to their future writing.

Objectives

- Students will understand the concept of conjunctions.
- Students will learn what coordinating, correlative, and subordinating conjunctions are.
- Students will understand the importance of conjunctions to strong writing.
- Students will be able to use coordinating, correlative, and subordinating conjunctions in their writing and reflect on the importance of doing so.

DOI: 10.4324/9781003610656-15

Time Frame

Two class periods.

Background Knowledge Required

Students will need to be familiar with the concept of sentences.

Materials Needed

- Figures 5.1.1–5.1.5, which are available in the plan, in Appendix B: Reproducible Graphic Organizers, and on the book's website.
- A board, projector, or piece of chart paper for displaying information.
- Paper for students' writing.

Detailed Plan

Day One
1. Introduction
To begin this instructional process, you'll introduce students to the topic of conjunctions, present the key question for the first day of work on this topic, and share the day's agenda.

"Let's begin our work on conjunctions, tools that authors use to connect statements. We'll focus on three conjunction types: coordinating, correlative, and subordinating. Today's key questions are:

- What are conjunctions?
- Why are conjunctions important to strong writing?
- How do writers use coordinating, correlative, and subordinating conjunctions?

The agenda for day's work is:

- Conjunction mini-lesson
- Mentor text examples
- Mentor text discussion and analysis activities
- Exit question"

I recommend displaying the day's questions and agenda items while reading them to students.

2. Conjunction Mini-Lesson

Next, you'll teach a mini-lesson about conjunctions. In it, you'll describe what conjunctions are, introduce coordinating, correlative, and subordinating conjunctions, discuss features and examples of those conjunction types, and share information about the importance of conjunctions.

"In this mini-lesson, we'll think about key information about conjunctions. We'll continue to explore these ideas as we continue to learn about this topic. Conjunctions are grammatical tools that authors use to connect statements. There are three types of conjunctions that we'll explore: coordinating, correlative, and subordinating conjunctions. Let's look at a chart containing information about these conjunction types."

Conjunction Type	What It Is	Examples	Used in a Sentence
Coordinating conjunction	A word that connects related statements of equal importance.	for, and, nor, but, or, yet, so	Brody cooked the hamburgers, **and** Sawyer made the salad.
Correlative conjunction	A two-part structure that connects related statements of equal importance.	both-and, not only-but also, either-or, neither-nor	**Either** we will watch the movie today, **or** we will watch it tomorrow.
Subordinating conjunction	A word or phrase that connects two statements when one statement is dependent on the other.	after, although, because, before, if, since, until, while	**Since** the ground is covered with snow, we will go sledding.

Figure 5.1.1 Coordinating, Correlative, and Subordinating Conjunction Information

I recommend displaying this chart and reading its contents aloud while students follow along.

"Let's now think about why conjunctions are important to strong writing. Conjunctions are important to strong writing because they help make writing easy to read by linking ideas together. Without conjunctions, writers would have to write a lot of short and choppy sentences. Writers can connect their ideas with conjunctions."

3. Mentor Text Examples

You'll share with students published examples of coordinating, correlative, and subordinating conjunctions. This helps students see authentic examples of how these concepts are used.

"We'll look together at how published authors use coordinating, correlative, and subordinating conjunctions in their writing by examining a chart that contains published examples of each of these conjunction types."

Published Coordinating Conjunction Example	**Published Correlative Conjunction Example**	**Published Subordinating Conjunction Example**
"My voice catches in my throat, **and** I stumble over my words" (Keller, 2020, p. 6). From *When You Trap a Tiger* by Tae Keller	"You **either** like someone **or** you don't" (Medina, 2018, p. 126). From *Merci Suárez Changes Gears* by Meg Medina	"**Since** my mom and stepdad thought it was gross, we usually only got those toppings on half a pie" (Marks, 2020, p. 5). From *From the Desk of Zoe Washington* by Janae Marks

Figure 5.1.2 Published Coordinating, Correlative, and Subordinating Conjunction Examples

I suggest displaying these sentences and reading them aloud. While reading each sentence, I recommend identifying the relevant conjunction type in the sentence and talking with students about why each conjunction is an example of its type.

4. Mentor Text Discussion and Analysis Activities

Here, you'll lead students through activities that will help them understand the importance of the conjunctions in the mentor text examples.

"Now that we've seen published examples of coordinating, correlative, and subordinating conjunctions, we'll discuss the importance of each of those conjunction types to the sentences to the sentences in which they were used. We'll look again at each mentor text. You'll think about the importance of the conjunction type featured in the sentence and share ideas with a partner. Then, we'll record insights on a chart I'll display."

Coordinating Conjunction Mentor Text	Importance of the Coordinating Conjunction to the Sentence
"My voice catches in my throat, **and** I stumble over my words" (Keller, 2020, p. 6).	

Figure 5.1.3 Coordinating Conjunction Analysis Chart

I suggest displaying this chart, reading the sentence aloud, and asking students to talk with partners about the importance of the coordinating conjunction in this sentence. As students talk, I move around the classroom to provide support. Afterward, I ask volunteers to share ideas, which I record on the chart. When students share, I look for answers that highlight how the coordinating conjunction connects the statements made in the sentence.

"Next, we'll think about the correlative conjunction mentor text. I'll display the correlative conjunction example, and you'll talk with a partner about the importance of the correlative conjunction to the sentence. We'll then record responses on a chart."

Correlative Conjunction Mentor Text	Importance of the Correlative Conjunction to the Sentence
"You **either** like someone **or** you don't" (Medina, 2018, p. 126).	

Figure 5.1.4 Correlative Conjunction Analysis Chart

I recommend displaying this information, reading the mentor text aloud, asking students to discuss in pairs the importance of the correlative conjunction to the sentence, and circulating the classroom while they do so to provide support.

As volunteers share, I record highlights on the chart. I look for responses that address how the correlative conjunction links the points made in the sentence and uses a two-part structure to do so. I also encourage students to think about how this two-part structure clearly shows how the information in the sentence is connected.

"Let's focus now on our subordinating conjunction mentor text. We'll look at the subordinating conjunction example, you'll talk to a partner about the importance of the subordinating conjunction to the sentence, and I'll record responses on a chart."

Subordinating Conjunction Mentor Text	**Importance of the Subordinating Conjunction to the Sentence**
"**Since** my mom and stepdad thought it was gross, we usually only got those toppings on half a pie" (Marks, 2020, p. 5).	

Figure 5.1.5 Subordinating Conjunction Analysis Chart

You'll display this chart, read the example aloud, and ask students to talk with partners about the importance of the subordinating conjunction to the sentence. While students talk, I recommend moving around the classroom to provide support. Then, you'll ask volunteers to share, listing insights on the chart. I look for responses that identify how the subordinating conjunction is important because it connects ideas in the sentences and shows that the first statement gives background information about the second one.

5. Exit Question

To conclude this class period, students answer an exit question about conjunctions.

"You'll now write an answer to an exit question conjunctions. I'll ask for volunteers to share responses, and I'll collect everyone's answers. The exit question 'Why are conjunctions important tools for writers to use?'"

I like to display this question while students write their responses. I recommend reviewing students' written responses to evaluate their understanding of conjunctions. If students show any confusion, you can address this in future instruction.

Day Two
1. Introduction
You'll begin the second instructional day on conjunctions by discussing how the day's work will build on the previous day, presenting the day's questions, and sharing the agenda.

"Excellent job working on conjunctions yesterday! You learned what conjunctions are, explored the features of coordinating, correlative, and subordinating conjunctions, considered their importance, examined and analyzed published examples of these conjunction types, and answered an exit question about why conjunctions are important tools for writers to use. Today, we'll think even further about conjunctions by reviewing key information about them, creating our own sentences that use coordinating, correlative, and subordinating conjunctions, reflecting on the benefits of using each type, and answering an exit question about how conjunctions can be important to your future writing. Today's key questions are:

- How can we use coordinating, correlative, and subordinating conjunctions in our writing?
- Why are each of these conjunction types important to the effectiveness of our writing?

Today's agenda is:

- Conjunction review
- Writing activity
- Reflection
- Exit question"

I recommend displaying these questions and this agenda while sharing the information.

2. Conjunction Review
Here, you'll review significant information about conjunctions discussed the previous day.

"Let's review key information about conjunctions that we discussed yesterday. First, let's recap what conjunctions are. As we talked about yesterday, conjunctions are grammatical tools that authors use to connect statements. Conjunctions are important to strong writing because they help make writing easy to read by linking ideas together. Without conjunctions, writers would have to write a lot of short, choppy sentences."

"Yesterday, we talked about three conjunction types: coordinating, correlative, and subordinating conjunctions. Let's review the chart we looked at yesterday that describes these conjunction types."

I recommend displaying Figure 5.1.1: Coordinating, Correlative, and Subordinating Conjunction Information, which you shared in the previous day's conjunction mini-lesson, and reviewing the descriptions, examples, and usage of each conjunction type. If students demonstrated any confusion about conjunctions in the previous lesson, this is a great time to clarify any misunderstandings.

3. Writing Activity

Next, students apply their knowledge of coordinating, correlative, and subordinating conjunctions by creating sentences containing these conjunction types.

"We're going to put our knowledge conjunctions into action in our writing! You'll write three sentences: one that contains a coordinating conjunction, one that contains a correlative conjunction two-part structure, and one that contains a subordinating conjunction. Before you write, I'll share my examples. For my coordinating conjunction sentence, I wrote 'Jane ran the race, but Michael did not.' For my correlative conjunction sentence, I wrote 'Either the dog is in the house, or he is in the backyard.' My subordinating conjunction sentence is 'Because it rained last night, the baseball game is postponed.'"

You can share these examples with students or create your own. I recommend displaying the sentences while sharing them with students.

"You'll now write your own examples. Remember that you'll create three sentences. One will contain a coordinating conjunction, one will contain a correlative conjunction two-part structure, and one will contain a subordinating conjunction. I'll check in with you while you write."

While students write, I suggest moving around the room to monitor their progress and support their work.

"Great work writing those sentences! Let's have two volunteers share their sentences and tell us the conjunction type used in each one."

As students share, I like to praise strong examples of conjunction use and provide any needed support.

4. Reflection

Students now revisit the sentences they created in the writing activity and reflect on the importance of each conjunction type to the sentence in which it was used.

"It's now time for our reflective activity. You'll re-read the three sentences you just wrote and answer the following reflection question for each sentence:

'Why is the conjunction type you used in the sentence you wrote important to its effectiveness?'"

I suggest displaying the reflection question while reading it.

"Before you start, I'll share my reflections for the sentences I wrote. For my coordinating conjunction sentence 'Jane ran the race, but Michael did not,' my reflection is 'The coordinating conjunction is important to this sentence because it connects the statements about running the race and helps the information in the sentence flow together.' For my correlative conjunction sentence 'Either the dog is in the house, or he is in the backyard,' my reflection is 'The correlative conjunction pair is important to this sentence because it links the ideas I share here about the dog's location. Also, the two-part structure of the pair clearly shows how the information in the sentence is connected.' For my subordinating conjunction sentence 'Because it rained last night, the baseball game is postponed,' my reflection is 'The subordinating conjunction is important to this sentence because it connects the two statement about last night's rain with the statement about the baseball game being postponed while also showing that the first statement gives background information about the second one.'"

You can share these reflections with students if you use the same examples. If you create new examples, you can share reflections that correspond with them.

"It's your turn! Revisit your sentences and write an answer to the question 'Why is the conjunction type you used in the sentence you wrote important to its effectiveness?' for each."

As students write, I circulate the classroom, providing encouragement and support.

"We'll now have two volunteers share their sentences and reflections aloud. Afterward, everyone will turn in their sentences and reflections."

While students share, I call attention to strong reflections and clarify any confusion.

5. Exit Question

This instructional process finishes with students answering an exit question about the importance of conjunctions to their future writing.

"We'll wrap up our work with an exit question on conjunctions. You'll write an answer, two volunteers will share, and everyone will submit their answers. The exit question is 'How can the use of conjunctions be important to your future writing?'"

I recommend displaying this question while students write their responses. When they share answers, I suggest praising strong statements and providing any clarification needed.

Differentiation Suggestions

There are numerous ways to differentiate this lesson:

- Students can read additional mentor texts containing the conjunction types addressed in the lesson to show them additional published examples of these concepts.
- Students can work with conjunction mentor types on a range of reading levels to help them find texts that fit well for them.
- Students can create additional passages that contain conjunctions. In these passages, students can use various examples of each conjunction type.

Assessment

I recommend assessing students' knowledge of conjunctions in the following ways:

- Students' exit question responses.
    - Students' answers to the exit questions in this lesson sequence provide important insights into their understandings of conjunctions. When evaluating students' responses to the day-one exit question, "Why are conjunctions important tools for writers to use?," I assess how effectively they explain that conjunctions are important tools for writers to use because they link ideas together and make writing easy to read. When assessing students' answers to the day-two exit question, "How can the use of conjunctions be important to your future writing?," I evaluate how well students discuss that they can use conjunctions in their future writing to connect ideas, make their work easy to read, and avoid writing a lot of short, choppy sentences.
- Students' written examples and reflections.
    - The example sentences that students create coordinating, correlative, and subordinating conjunctions and the corresponding reflections also provide excellent opportunities to assess student knowledge. When evaluating students' sentences, I determine if they used the appropriate conjunction type in each sentence and if they did so correctly. When assessing students' reflections, I consider the ideas and details present in their discussion of the importance of the conjunction type used in each sentence.

Notes

◆ What worked when teaching this lesson?

◆ What might you adapt or change the next time you teach it?

References

Keller, T. (2020). *When you trap a tiger*. Yearling.
Marks, J. (2020). *From the desk of Zoe Washington*. Katherine Tegen Books.
Medina, M. (2018). *Merci Suárez changes gears*. Candlewick Press.

LESSON 5.2

Showing Emotion

Interjections

Overview

This lesson focuses on the concept of interjections, single words or short phrases that writers use to show emotion. The lesson covers two class periods. On the first day, students will learn what interjections are, examine examples of them, explore how they're used in published writing, and reflect on why writers use them. One the second day, students will review key ideas about interjections, use them in their own writing, and think about the importance of the interjections to the pieces they wrote. The sequence concludes with students answering an exit question about the importance of interjections to strong writing.

Objectives

- Students will understand the concept of interjections.
- Students will understand the importance of interjections to strong writing.
- Students will be able to use interjections in their writing and reflect on the importance of doing so.

Time Frame

Two class periods.

DOI: 10.4324/9781003610656-16

Background Knowledge Required

Students will need to understand the concept of sentences when adding interjections to sentences.

Materials Needed

- Figures 5.2.1–5.2.4, which are available in the lesson plan, in Appendix B: Reproducible Graphic Organizers, and electronically on the book's website.
- A board, projector, or piece of chart paper for displaying information.
- Paper for students' writing activities.

Detailed Plan

Day One
1. Introduction
You'll introduce this instructional process by letting students know they'll be studying interjections, sharing the questions about conjunctions they'll consider that day, and presenting the agenda for the class period.

"We're going to learn about the grammatical concept of interjections, which are single words or short phrases that writers use to show emotion. We'll explore these key questions today:

- What are interjections?
- Why are interjections important to strong writing?

Today's agenda is:

- Interjection mini-lesson
- Mentor text example
- Mentor text discussion and analysis activities
- Exit question"

I suggest displaying the key questions and agenda items while reading them aloud.

2. Interjection Mini-Lesson
In this mini-lesson, you'll share key ideas about interjections, provide examples of them, and describe their importance to strong writing.

"Let's get into our mini-lesson on interjections. I'll share key information on this grammatical concept, which will get us started thinking about interjections. We'll continue to think about these ideas as we work on this topic."

"We'll start by thinking about what interjections are. Interjections are single words or short phrases that writers use to show emotion. Some single words that can function as interjections are 'wow,' yay,' and 'ouch.' Some short phrases that can function as interjections are 'my gosh,' 'no way,' and 'oh my.' Interjections often are used at the beginning of sentences, such as 'Wow, that was a great game,' or 'Oh my! It snowed a lot last night!'"

"Interjections can be used with commas or exclamation points, depending on how much emotion the writer wants to express. Exclamation points are used to stronger emotions than commas are. Interjections are important to strong writing because they can help a writer or a character show the emotion they're feeling, which can enhance the reader's understanding of the piece. For example, if a writer wanted to show happiness about eating pizza for dinner, they could use the interjection 'yay' to say 'Yay! We're having pizza for dinner!' Let's look at a chart that contains key information about interjections."

Grammatical Concept	What Are Interjections?	What Are Some Examples of Interjections	What Are Some Ways Interjections Can Look in Writing?	Why Are Interjections Important to Strong Writing?
Interjections	Interjections are single words or short phrases that writers use to show emotion.	Some examples of single-word interjections: wow, yay, ouch Some examples of short-phrase interjections: my gosh, no way, oh my	**Wow**, that was a great game. **Yay**! We're having pizza for dinner! **My gosh**, that's a heavy suitcase. **Oh my**! It snowed a lot last night.	Interjections are important to strong writing because they can help a writer or character show the emotion they're feeling, which can enhance the reader's understanding of the piece.

Figure 5.2.1 Interjection Information

I recommend displaying this chart and reading its contents aloud while students follow along.

3. Mentor Text Example

You'll now share with students a published example of interjection use. By looking at a published mentor text example of this concept, students can see how interjections are used in authentic writing and deepen their awareness of this topic.

"Now, we'll look at a published example of an interjection being used. In the book *The Braid Girls*, author Sherri Winston (2023) uses the interjection 'Sweet!' in the excerpt *'Sweet!* That's when my braces come off!' (p. 6). In our next activity, we'll think about the importance of this interjection."

I suggest displaying the mentor text example and reading it aloud for students.

4. Mentor Text Discussion and Analysis Activities

Next, you'll lead students through activities designed to help them consider the importance of the interjection used in the mentor text example. This work can develop students' awareness of the impact that interjections can have on writing.

"We're going to think about why the interjection 'Sweet!' is important to the mentor text example we read from *The Braid Girls*. To start, we'll compare the original text with a revised version that does not contain the interjection."

Original Text	Revised Version with Interjection Removed
"*Sweet!* That's when my braces come off!" (Winston, 2023, p. 6).	That's when my braces come off!

Figure 5.2.2 Original Text vs. Revised Version With Interjection Removed

I like to display this chart and read the examples to students while they follow along.

"Please talk with a partner about these two questions: How is the sentence different without the interjection 'Sweet!'? and Why do you think the author used this interjection in the text? After you talk with your partner, volunteers will share with the class. I'll write responses on a graphic organizer."

Reflection Question One	Reflection Question Two
How is the sentence different without the interjection "Sweet!"?	Why do you think the author used this interjection in the text?

Figure 5.2.3 Interjection Reflection Questions Graphic Organizer

I suggest projecting this chart or recreating it on chart paper. When students share their answers, I like to record highlights of their responses on the chart.

5. Exit Question

To conclude this class period, students answer an exit question about why writers use interjections.

"We'll finish today's work on interjections with an exit question. You'll write an answer to the question on a piece of paper, and then I'll ask for two volunteers to share responses. After that, I'll collect everyone's answers. The exit question 'Why would writers use interjections in their writing?'"

I recommend displaying the exit question while students write their answers. I review students' answers to assess their understandings of interjections. This assessment can guide future instruction.

Day Two
1. Introduction

To begin the second day of work on interjections, you'll explain how what students will do that day builds on the previous day's work, present the day's key questions, and share the agenda.

"Great work on interjections yesterday! In yesterday's class, you learned key ideas about interjections, looked at an interjection mentor text from the book *The Braid Girls* by Sherri Winston (2023), considered the importance of the interjection 'Sweet!' to that mentor text, and responded to an exit question about why writers would use interjections in their writing. Today, we'll explore interjections even further. First, we'll review important interjection information. Next, we'll use interjections in our writing and reflect on their importance. We'll conclude with an exit question about why interjections are important tools for strong writing. Today's key questions are:

- How can we use interjections in our writing?
- How can interjections show emotion in our writing?

Today's agenda is:

- Interjection review
- Writing activity
- Reflection
- Exit question"

I suggest displaying these questions and agenda items while sharing them with students.

2. Interjection Review

Here, you'll review key information, examples, and ideas about interjections discussed the previous day.

"Let's review key ideas about interjections that we discussed yesterday. We'll look together at a chart that reviews what interjections are, shares some examples of them, discusses why they're important to strong writing, and provides a published example of their use."

What Are Interjections?	What Are Some Examples of Interjections?	Why Are Interjections Important to Strong Writing?	What Is a Published Example of Interjection Use?
Interjections are single words or short phrases that writers use to show emotion.	Some examples of single-word interjections: wow, yay, ouch Some examples of short-phrase interjections: my gosh, no way, oh my	Interjections are important to strong writing because they can help a writer or character show the emotion they're feeling, which can enhance the reader's understanding of the piece.	"*Sweet!* That's when my braces come off!" (Winston, 2023, p. 6).

Figure 5.2.4 Interjection Review Information

I recommend displaying this chart and reading the information on it aloud. I suggest also using this time to discuss any aspects of interjections that may have confused students on the previous day.

3. Writing Activity

In this writing activity, students apply the concept of interjections to their writing. They create a passage that uses an interjection to show emotion.

"We'll now put our knowledge of interjections into action in our writing! You'll write a one- or two-sentence passage that uses an interjection to show emotion. That emotion can be positive or negative—it's up to you and how you use the interjection."

"Before you start, I'll share an example passage I wrote that uses an interjection: 'Hooray! Baseball season starts today!' I used the interjection 'Hooray!' to show my excitement about the start of baseball season and underlined that interjection in the passage."

You can use this interjection example when you teach this lesson, or you can create your own interjection example.

"It's your turn. You'll create a passage that uses an interjection, and you'll underline the interjection like I did in my example. I'll ask you to share your work with a partner. Then, volunteers will share with the class."

While students write, I suggest moving through the classroom to provide support and recognize strong work.

"Good job creating those passages. Please share your work with a partner and identify the interjection in your passage."

As students share with partners, I recommend listening to their statements and providing feedback.

"Let's now take two volunteers to share their passage and identify the interjection they used."

I also like to use this time to identify strong examples and provide relevant support.

4. Reflection

In this reflective activity, students return to the passage they wrote and reflect on the importance of the interjection to that passage.

"Now that you've written a passage containing an interjection, you'll reread that passage and reflect on the importance of the interjection you used. You'll then write an answer to the exit question 'Why is the interjection you used important to the passage you created?'"

I recommend displaying this question while reading it aloud.

"Before you do this, I'll share my reflection about my passage 'Hooray! Baseball season starts today!' My reflection is 'The interjection hooray is important to my passage because it shows my excitement about baseball season starting. If I didn't use this interjection, I wouldn't express as much emotion in the passage as I currently do. The interjection helps the reader understand my excitement about the start of baseball season.'"

If you use this example with your students, you can share the reflection with them. If you create your own passage that uses an interjection, I recommend sharing a reflection that corresponds with that passage.

"You'll now write your reflection. Reread your passage that uses an interjection and write an answer to the question 'Why is the interjection you used important to the passage you created?'"

As students work on their reflections, I suggest circulating the room to check on their work and share feedback.

"Good work answering the reflection question. Now, please share your reflection with a partner. They'll then share theirs with you."

While students share with partners, I like to again move around the classroom to hear their insights and respond to their work.

"Let's now have two volunteers share their reflection question responses verbally with the rest of the class. Then, everyone will turn in their reflections and the passages they wrote during the writing activity."

During this time when students share, I recommend identifying strong insights and providing additional explanation when needed.

5. Exit Question

This instructional process concludes with students responding to an exit question about the importance of interjections.

"We'll conclude our work on interjections with an exit question. You'll write an answer to an exit question on interjections. Then, I'll ask for two volunteers to share their ideas with the class. Afterward, I'll collect everyone's written responses. The exit question is 'Why are interjections important tools for strong writing?'"

I recommend displaying this exit question while reading it aloud. When volunteers share answers, I suggest recognizing strong insights and commenting further on any responses that can be developed in more detail.

Differentiation Suggestions

This lesson can be differentiated in a number of ways:

- Students can explore additional interjection mentor texts, providing them with additional examples of interjections in published works.
- Students can engage with interjection mentor texts on a variety of reading levels, helping them work with texts that best fit them.
- Students can create multiple passages that contain interjections and use different interjections in those passages.

Assessment

I recommend assessing students' knowledge of interjections and their work in this lesson sequence in the following ways:

- Students' exit question responses.
  - Students' answers to the two exit questions in this instructional process can show their knowledge of interjections and the importance of this concept to strong writing. When evaluating students' answers to the day-one exit question, "Why would writers use interjections in their writing?," I recommend assessing how well students explain that writers use interjections

to show emotion in their works. When assessing students' responses to the day-two exit question, "Why are interjections important tools for strong writing?," I suggest evaluating how well students express that interjections are important tools for strong writing because they can help a writer or character show the emotion they're feeling, which can enhance the reader's understanding of the piece.

- Students' written passages and corresponding reflections.
  - The written passages that students create in which they use interjections to show emotion and the corresponding reflections they compose are also excellent ways to evaluate their understanding of interjections. When evaluating students' written passages, I assess if they used an interjection in the passage, if the interjection is used with a comma or exclamation point, and if the interjection expresses emotion about the information in the passage. When assessing students' responses to the reflection question, I consider the ideas and details they use when discussing the importance of the interjection to the passage they wrote.

Notes

- What worked when teaching this lesson?

- What might you adapt or change the next time you teach it?

Reference

Winston, S. (2023). *The braid girls*. Little, Brown and Company.

LESSON 5.3

Pronouns and Clarity

Pronoun-Antecedent Agreement

Overview

This lesson addresses the concept of pronoun-antecedent agreement, which is the idea that pronouns need to clearly refer to the nouns that they represent by matching in number, person, and gender as relevant to a statement. The lesson spans two class periods. On day one, students will learn what pronoun-antecedent agreement is, explore examples of it, examine how it appears in published writing, and consider its importance. On day two, students will review key features of pronoun-antecedent agreement, apply the concept to their own writing, and reflect on how pronoun-antecedent agreement is important to the effectiveness of their works. At the conclusion of the lesson sequence, students will consider how this concept can be important to their future writing.

Objectives

- Students will understand the concept of pronoun-antecedent agreement.
- Students will understand the importance of pronoun-antecedent agreement to strong writing.
- Students will be able to use pronoun-antecedent in their writing and reflect on the importance of doing so.

DOI: 10.4324/9781003610656-17

Time Frame

Two class periods.

Background Knowledge Required

Students will need background knowledge of nouns and pronouns. The concept of pronouns is also discussed in the day-one mini-lesson.

Materials Needed

- Figures 5.3.1– 5.3.4, which are available in the lesson plan, in Appendix B: Reproducible Graphic Organizers, and electronically on the book's website.
- A board, projector, or piece of chart paper for displaying information.
- Paper for students' writing.

Detailed Plan
1. Introduction
You'll begin this instructional process by introducing students to the topic of pronoun-antecedent agreement, sharing the key questions for the first day of work on this concept, and presenting the day's agenda.

"Today, we'll explore the grammatical concept of pronoun-antecedent agreement. We'll consider these questions:

- What is pronoun-antecedent agreement?
- What does pronoun-antecedent look like?
- Why is pronoun-antecedent agreement important to strong writing?

Here is today's agenda:

- Pronoun-antecedent agreement mini-lesson
- Mentor text example
- Mentor text discussion and analysis activities
- Exit question"

I suggest displaying these questions and agenda items while reading them aloud.

2. Pronoun-Antecedent Agreement Mini-Lesson
Next, you'll conduct a mini-lesson on pronoun-antecedent agreement. In it, you'll introduce students to what pronoun-antecedent agreement is, share key information related to it, provide examples of it, and discuss its importance.

"I'm going to share important ideas about pronoun-antecedent agreement in this mini-lesson. This will be the first step in our work together on this topic. Let's begin by discussing pronouns and antecedents. Pronouns are words that take the place of a noun. Some examples of pronouns are *she, he, they, we, it, her, him, them*, and *us*. Antecedents are nouns that pronouns represent. They often come before the pronouns that refer to them. For example, in the sentence 'The dogs wanted to rest, so they sat down in the yard,' 'they' is a pronoun and 'the dogs' is the antecedent."

I recommend writing this sentence on the board while reading it.

"Pronoun-antecedent agreement is when pronouns clearly refer to the nouns they represent by matching in number, person, and gender as relevant to a statement. Problems with pronoun-antecedent agreement arise if it's not clear what a pronoun refers to. Our example sentence about the dogs has pronoun-antecedent agreement in both number and person. The pronoun 'they' and the antecedent 'the dogs' agree in number because 'the dogs' is plural and 'they' is used as a plural pronoun in this sentence. The pronoun and antecedent in this sentence also agree in person—the antecedent 'the dogs' is described in the third person, and the pronoun 'they' is also in the third person. If I said 'The dogs wanted to rest, so she sat down in the yard,' my sentence wouldn't have pronoun-antecedent agreement because I would be using the singular pronoun 'she' to refer to the plural antecedent 'the dogs.' In this case, the pronoun and antecedent would not agree in number. Pronoun-antecedent agreement is important to strong writing because it helps readers clearly understand what the writer is trying to express. If a piece of writing has problems with pronoun-antecedent agreement, readers could be distracted by those problems or misunderstand the information in the piece. Let's look at a chart that contains key information about pronoun-antecedent agreement."

Grammatical Concept	What Is Pronoun-Antecedent Agreement?	What Is an Example of Pronoun-Antecedent Agreement?	Why Is Pronoun-Antecedent Agreement Important to Strong Writing?
Pronoun-antecedent agreement	Pronoun-antecedent agreement is when pronouns clearly refer to the nouns they represent by matching in number, person, and gender as relevant to a statement.	The dogs wanted to rest, so they sat down in the yard. Note: In this sentence, the pronoun "they" agrees with the antecedent "the dogs" in number and in person.	Pronoun-antecedent agreement is important to strong writing because it helps readers clearly understand what the writer is trying to express. If a piece of writing has problems with pronoun-antecedent agreement, readers could be distracted by those problems or misunderstand the information in the piece.

Figure 5.3.1 Pronoun-Antecedent Agreement Information

I suggest displaying this chart while discussing its contents with students.

3. Mentor Text Example

In this part of the lesson, you'll share with students a published example of pronoun-antecedent agreement. This shows students an authentic example of what pronoun-antecedent agreement looks like and prepares them for future work on the topic.

"Let's take a look at a published example of pronoun antecedent agreement. In the book *The Way Home Looks Now*, author Wendy Wan-Long Shang (2015) uses clear pronoun-antecedent agreement between the pronoun 'it' and the antecedent 'jean jacket' in the sentence 'I watched him fold his jean jacket and put it in his duffel bag' (p. 35). In this sentence, the pronoun and antecedent agree in number and in person. They agree in number because 'it' is a singular pronoun that refers to the singular antecedent 'jean jacket.' They agree in person because 'jean jacket' is a third-person antecedent and 'it' is a third-person pronoun."

I recommend displaying this mentor text example while sharing it with students.

4. Mentor Text Discussion and Analysis Activities

During this section of the lesson, you'll discuss the pronoun-antecedent mentor text with students and lead them through activities designed to help them consider the importance of pronoun-antecedent agreement to the effectiveness of the piece.

"We'll now work together to think about why the pronoun-antecedent agreement is important to the mentor text example from *The Way Home Looks Now*. Let's first compare the original text to a revised version without pronoun-antecedent agreement. In the revised version, the pronoun 'it' is replaced with the pronoun 'them.' In this revised example, 'jean jacket' is still a singular antecedent, but 'them' is used here as a plural pronoun that would refer to multiple things, so the pronoun and antecedent do not agree in number in the revised version."

Original Text	Revised Version Without Pronoun-Antecedent Agreement
"I watched him fold his jean jacket and put **it** in his duffel bag" (Wan-Long Shang, 2015, p. 35).	I watched him fold his jean jacket and put **them** in his duffel bag.

Figure 5.3.2 Original Text vs. Revised Version Without Pronoun-Antecedent Agreement

I suggest displaying this chart and reading both examples aloud while students follow along.

"Next, please talk with a partner about these questions: How is the sentence different without pronoun-antecedent agreement? and Why is the pronoun-antecedent agreement important to the effectiveness of the original sentence? After you discuss these questions with a partner, volunteers will share with the class. I'll then record responses on a graphic organizer."

Reflection Question One	Reflection Question Two
How is the sentence different without pronoun-antecedent agreement?	Why is the pronoun-antecedent agreement important to the effectiveness of the original sentence?

Figure 5.3.3 Pronoun-Antecedent Agreement Reflection Question Graphic Organizer

I recommend displaying this chart while students talk with partners. When students share responses with the class, I like to record highlights of those responses on the chart. As they share their insights, I suggest calling attention to especially strong responses and providing additional explanation and support if needed.

5. Exit Question

This class period concludes with students answering a question on the importance of pronoun-antecedent agreement to strong writing.

"To conclude today's work on pronoun-antecedent agreement, you'll answer an exit question about this concept. You'll write your answer on a piece of paper, two volunteers will share their responses, and I'll collect everyone's answers. The exit question is 'Why is pronoun-antecedent agreement important to strong writing?'"

I suggest displaying this question while students write their answers. I recommend reviewing students' responses after you collect them to assess their understandings of the topic. This information can inform your future instruction.

Day Two
1. Introduction
To begin the second day of work on pronoun-antecedent agreement, you'll discuss how the day's lesson builds from the previous day's work, present the day's key questions, and share the agenda.

"Excellent job yesterday on pronoun-antecedent agreement! We discussed key information about pronoun-antecedent agreement, looked at a published example of this concept from the book *The Way Home Looks Now* by Wendy Wan-Long Shang (2015), analyzed the significance of the pronoun-antecedent agreement to that example, and answered an exit question about why pronoun-antecedent agreement is important to strong writing. Today, we'll explore pronoun-antecedent agreement even further. We'll first review key points about this concept. Then, we'll apply pronoun-antecedent agreement to our own writing and reflect on why this concept is important to the effectiveness of our works. We'll conclude with an exit question about the importance of pronoun-antecedent agreement to our future writing. Today's key questions are:

- How can we apply pronoun-antecedent agreement to our writing?
- Why is pronoun-antecedent agreement important to the effectiveness of our writing?

Here is today's agenda:

- Pronoun-antecedent agreement review
- Writing activity
- Reflection
- Exit question"

I recommend displaying the key questions and agenda items while sharing them with students.

2. Pronoun-Antecedent Review
Here, you'll review key information and examples from the previous day's work on pronoun-antecedent agreement.

"Let's review important information about pronoun-antecedent agreement we discussed yesterday. We'll look at a chart that reviews what pronoun antecedent agreement is, describes its importance to strong writing, and provides a published example of pronoun-antecedent agreement, and explains why pronoun-antecedent agreement is present in the example."

What Is Pronoun-Antecedent Agreement?	Why Is Pronoun-Antecedent Agreement Important to Strong Writing?	What Is a Published Example of Pronoun-Antecedent Agreement?	Why Is Pronoun-Antecedent Agreement Present in This Example?
Pronoun-antecedent agreement is when pronouns clearly refer to the nouns they represent by matching in number, person, and gender as relevant to a statement.	Pronoun-antecedent agreement is important to strong writing because it helps readers clearly understand what the writer is trying to express. If a piece of writing has problems with pronoun-antecedent agreement, readers could be distracted by those problems or misunderstand the information in the piece.	"I watched him fold his jean jacket and put **it** in his duffel bag" (Wan-Long Shang, 2015, p. 35).	In this example, the pronoun "it" and the antecedent "jean jacket" agree in number and person: "it" is a singular, third-person pronoun that refers to the singular, third-person antecedent "jean jacket."

Figure 5.3.4 Pronoun-Antecedent Agreement Review Information

I suggest displaying this chart and reading the information on it aloud while students follow along. If students had any difficulties understanding pronoun-antecedent agreement in the previous class, I recommend using this time to address anything about this concept that confused students.

3. Writing Activity
Next, students apply the concept of pronoun-antecedent to their writing by creating their own passages that contain pronoun-antecedent agreement and identifying why pronoun-antecedent agreement is present in the passage.

"Let's apply pronoun-antecedent agreement to our writing! You'll create a passage that contains pronoun-antecedent agreement and write why the passage contains pronoun-antecedent agreement."

"First, I'll share an example I wrote: 'The runners trained hard, and they did well in the race.' The passage contains pronoun-antecedent agreement because the pronoun and antecedent agree in number and in person. They agree in number because the antecedent 'the runners' is a plural antecedent, and the pronoun 'they' is used as a plural pronoun in this sentence. They agree in person because 'the runners' are referred to in the third-person, and 'they' is a third-person pronoun."

You can use this same example when you teach this lesson, or you can create your own to use.

"It's time now for you to create your own passage containing pronoun-antecedent agreement and write why the passage contains pronoun-antecedent agreement. You'll then share your example and explanation with a partner. Afterward, I'll ask for volunteers to share with the class."

During the time when students write, I recommend moving through the classroom to support their work.

"Now that you've created your passage and explanation, please share your work with a partner."

While students do this, I like to listen to their passages and explanations, providing feedback as relevant.

"We'll now have two volunteers share their passage and their explanation of why the passage contains pronoun-antecedent agreement."

As students share, I suggest recognizing strong work and providing additional clarification if needed.

4. Reflection

Here, students return to the passage they created during the writing activity and reflect on why the pronoun-antecedent agreement is important to the passage.

"Next, you'll reflect on the importance of the pronoun-antecedent agreement to the passage you wrote in our last activity. You'll write an answer to the question, 'Why is the pronoun-antecedent agreement in the passage you wrote important to the effectiveness of the passage?'"

I suggest displaying this question while reading it aloud.

"I'll share the reflection I wrote about my passage, 'The runners trained hard, and they did well in the race.' I said 'The pronoun-antecedent agreement between the pronoun they and the antecedent the runners is important to the effectiveness of the passage because it helps the reader clearly understand the information in the passage. The agreement between the pronoun and the antecedent makes clear to readers that I'm talking about multiple runners, and it also makes sure readers know that I'm using the third person when talking about the runners. If the pronoun they didn't agree with the antecedent the runners in number or in person, readers could misunderstand the piece or be distracted by the unclear writing.'"

You use this same reflection if you use this example of pronoun-antecedent agreement. If you create your own example, you'll share a reflection that aligns with it.

"You'll now revisit your passage and write an answer to the question 'Why is the pronoun-antecedent agreement in the passage you wrote important to the effectiveness of the passage?'"

When students write their answers, I recommend circulating the classroom to provide support and encouragement.

"Good job writing those responses. Now, share what you wrote with a partner."

As students *share responses with partners, I like to listen to what they share and offer feedback.*

"Let's take two volunteers to share their reflections verbally with the class. Afterward, everyone will turn in their reflections and their passages from the writing activity."

As volunteers share responses, I like to point out strong statements and provide explanation and clarification when relevant.

5. Exit Question

To close this instructional process, students answer an exit question about the importance of pronoun-antecedent agreement to their future writing.

"To conclude our work on pronoun-antecedent agreement, you'll write an answer to an exit question. Afterward, I'll ask for two volunteers to share their answers with the class. I'll then collect everyone's responses. The exit question is 'How can pronoun-antecedent agreement be important to your future writing?'"

I suggest displaying this question while reading it aloud. As volunteers share responses, I recommend recognizing insightful points and elaborating on any statements that can benefit from additional explanation.

Differentiation Suggestions

There are numerous differentiation options for this lesson:

- ◆ Students can explore additional pronoun-antecedent mentor texts, providing them with increased opportunities to see how published authors use these concepts.
- ◆ Students can engage with published examples that have a variety of forms of pronoun-antecedent to show different ways pronouns and antecedents can agree in number, person, and gender.

- Students can read pronoun-antecedent mentor texts on a range of reading levels.
- Students can write multiple passages containing pronoun-antecedent agreement in the writing activity.
- Students can create examples that represent different forms of pronoun-antecedent agreement.

Assessment

I suggest assessing students' understandings of pronoun-antecedent agreement and their work in this instructional process in the following ways:

- Students' exit question responses.
    - The two exit question responses students write during this lesson sequence provide important insights into their understandings of pronoun-antecedent agreement. When assessing students' answers to the day-one exit question, "Why is pronoun-antecedent agreement important to strong writing?," I recommend evaluating how well students explain that pronoun-antecedent is important because it helps readers clearly understand what a writer is trying to express. When evaluating students' answers to the day-two exit question, "How can pronoun-antecedent agreement be important to your future writing?," I suggest assessing how well students explain that pronoun-antecedent agreement can help readers of their works understand the information they are communicating and avoid distractions or misunderstandings that can come from problems with pronoun-antecedent agreement.
- Students' written passages and reflections.
    - I also recommend assessing students' knowledge of pronoun-antecedent agreement by reading their written passages from the writing activity and their corresponding reflections. When assessing students' written passages, I evaluate if the works contain pronoun and antecedent agreement, examine why the pronouns and antecedents agree, and determine if students correctly identified why their passages contained pronoun-antecedent agreement. When evaluating students' written reflections, I assess the insight and detail in their statements about why the pronoun-antecedent in the passage they wrote is important to its effectiveness.

Notes

♦ What worked when teaching this lesson?

♦ What might you adapt or change the next time you teach it?

Reference

Wan-Long Shang, W. (2015). *The way home looks now*. Scholastic.

LESSON 5.4

Beyond the Literal

Figurative Language

Overview

This lesson addresses the concept of figurative language, language that is not meant to be understood literally and provides description, emphasis, or expression to a piece of writing. It focuses on three types of figurative language: similes, metaphors, and personification. The lesson spans two class periods. On the first day, students will learn what figurative language is, see examples of it, explore how published writers use it, and consider the impact that figurative language can have on writing. On the second day, students will review key ideas about figurative language, use figurative language in their writing, and reflect on the impact of doing so. At the end of this instructional process, students answer an exit question about the importance of figurative language to strong writing.

Objectives

- Students will understand the concept of figurative language, with a focus on similes, metaphors, and personification.
- Students will understand the importance of figurative language to strong writing.
- Students will be able to use figurative language in their writing and reflect on the importance of doing so.

Time Frame

Two class periods.

Background Knowledge Required

No specific background knowledge is required for this lesson.

Materials Needed

- Figures 5.4.1– 5.4.7, which are available in the lesson plan, in Appendix B: Reproducible Graphic Organizers, and electronically on the book's website.
- A board, projector, or piece of chart paper for displaying information.
- Paper for students' writing.

Detailed Plan

Day One
1. Introduction
You'll introduce this lesson sequence by letting students know they'll be studying figurative language, identifying the forms of figurative language they'll explore, presenting the day's key questions, and sharing the agenda for the day.

"We're going to learn about figurative language, which is language that is not meant to be understood literally and provides description, emphasis, or expression to a piece of writing. We'll explore three types of figurative language: similes, metaphors, and personification. Here are the key questions for our work today:

- What is figurative language?
- What are the characteristics of similes, metaphors, and personification?
- Why is figurative language important to strong writing?

Today's agenda is:

- Figurative language mini-lesson
- Mentor text examples
- Mentor text discussion and analysis activities
- Exit question"

I suggest displaying these questions and agenda items while reading them aloud.

2. Figurative Language Mini-Lesson

You'll now teach a mini-lesson on key information regarding figurative language. In it, you'll introduce students to the concept of figurative language, discuss specific types of figurative language, provide examples, and describe the importance of the concept.

"In this mini-lesson, I'll share key information about figurative language. We'll continue to discuss and explore these ideas we work on this topic. Let's first talk about what figurative language is. Figurative language is language that is not meant to be understood literally and provides description, emphasis, or expression to a piece of writing. We're going to focus on three types of figurative language: similes, metaphors, and personification. Let's look at a chart that describes these three types of figurative language."

Type of Figurative Language	Definition	Example
Similes	Similes are comparisons of two different things using the words *like* or *as*.	She ran to her dog like a race car speeding to the finish line.
Metaphors	Metaphors are comparisons of two different things that state one thing is another.	The cup of warm, delicious soup is a big hug.
Personification	Personification is the giving of human qualities to a nonliving thing.	The beach was calling to her.

Figure 5.4.1 Information About Similes, Metaphors, and Personification

I recommend displaying this chart and reading it aloud while students follow along.
"Similes, metaphors, and personification are different in their specific characteristics, but they are also forms of figurative language that writers can use in their works. Figurative language is important to strong writing because it enhances the reader's understanding of what is being described and allows the author or character to express information in a way that is unique and memorable. For example, in the simile example from Figure 5.4.1, 'She ran to her dog like a race car speeding to the finish line,' the simile 'like race car speeding to the finish line' helps the reader understand how the character ran to her dog and does so in a unique and memorable way. If the sentence didn't contain figure language and instead read 'She ran quickly to her dog,' the text wouldn't have the same description or unique and memorable

expression. Let's now look at a chart that summarizes key points about figurative language."

Grammatical Concept	What Is Figurative Language?	What Are Some Types of Figurative Language?	Why Is Figurative Language Important to Strong Writing?
Figurative language	Figurative language is language that is not meant to be understood literally and provides description, emphasis, or expression to a piece of writing.	Some types of figurative language are similes, metaphors, and personification.	Figurative language is important to strong writing because it enhances the reader's understanding of what is being described and allows the author or character to express information in a way that is unique and memorable.

Figure 5.4.2 Figurative Language Information

I suggest displaying this chart and reading its contents aloud.

3. Mentor Text Examples

At this point in the lesson, you'll share with students a published example of a simile, a metaphor, and a personification. This shows students how these figurative language forms are used in authentic writing.

"We'll now look at published mentor text examples of figurative language. I'm going to show you a published example of a simile, a metaphor, and personification. Let's look at a chart containing these examples."

Simile Mentor Text	Metaphor Mentor Text	Personification Mentor Text
"She ran like a kite that had been let loose on a gusty day, gliding across the sky, not stopping until it reached a tree" (Holt, 2023, p. 5). From *The Hurricane Girls* by Kimberly Willis Holt	"… the ocean is a strong woman…" (Mendez, 2023, p. 9). From *Aniana del Mar Jumps In* by Jasminne Mendez	"The sun shrugs over the edge of the globe…" (Schmidt, 2023, p. 5). From *The Labors of Hercules Beal* by Gary D. Schmidt

Figure 5.4.3 Figurative Language Mentor Texts

I like to display these mentor text examples and read them aloud while students follow along. As I read the examples, I like to point out why each example contains figurative language. For example, I'll say that the simile example uses the word 'like' to compare the character's running ability to a flying kite, the metaphor example compares the ocean to a strong woman by saying one thing is the other, and the personification example gives the sun the ability to shrug.

4. Mentor Text Discussion and Analysis Activities

Here, you'll guide students through a discussion of the figurative language mentor texts and corresponding activities designed to help them think about the importance of the figurative language in those texts.

"Next, we'll think about the importance of the figurative language used in each of our mentor text examples. We'll look at each of our figurative language mentor texts compared with a revised version of each example that does not contain figurative language. After we look at each example, you'll discuss with a partner why you think the figure language is important to the original example. Volunteers will share with the class, and I'll record responses on a graphic organizer that I'll display. Let's start with the simile example. I'll display a graphic organizer containing our simile mentor text, a revised version without the simile, and a reflection question about the importance of the simile to the original example. After we read the information together, you'll discuss the reflection question with a partner, and I'll record responses from volunteers on the graphic organizer."

Original Text	Text Rewritten Without Simile	Reflection Question: Why Is the Simile Important to the Original Example?
"She ran like a kite that had been let loose on a gusty day, gliding across the sky, not stopping until it reached a tree" (Holt, 2023, p. 5).	She ran effortlessly.	

Figure 5.4.4 Simile Analysis Graphic Organizer

I suggest displaying this chart, reading the examples aloud, and asking students to talk with partners about the importance of the simile to the original example. While they talk, I move around the room and *support their insights. After that, I ask for volunteers to share and record highlights from their responses on the chart.*

"Let's now think about our metaphor example. I'll display a graphic organizer containing the metaphor mentor text, a revised version of the sentence without the metaphor, and a reflection question that asks why the metaphor is important to the original example. We'll read the information together and you'll discuss the reflection question with a partner. Afterward, I'll write volunteers' insights on the graphic organizer."

Original Text	Text Rewritten Without Metaphor	Reflection Question: Why Is the Metaphor Important to the Original Example?
"…the ocean is a strong woman…" (Mendez, 2023, p. 9).	The ocean is powerful.	

Figure 5.4.5 Metaphor Analysis Graphic Organizer

I recommend displaying the graphic organizer, sharing its contents aloud, and asking that students talk with partners about the reflection question. As they do so, I like to circulate the classroom to provide feedback on their ideas. I then call for volunteers to share their ideas; I write points from those responses in the third column.

"We'll focus now on analyzing our personification example. I'll share a graphic organizer containing the personification mentor text and a revised version that doesn't contain personification, and a reflection question about the importance of personification to the original text. I'll read the text aloud while you follow along, you'll discuss the reflection question with a partner, and then volunteers will share while I write their responses on the graphic organizer."

Original Text	**Text Rewritten Without Personification**	**Reflection Question: Why Is Personification Important to the Original Example?**
"The sun shrugs over the edge of the globe…" (Schmidt, 2023, p. 5).	The sun moves over the edge of the globe.	

Figure 5.4.6 Personification Analysis Graphic Organizer

You'll share this graphic organizer with students, read the information aloud, and ask students to talk with partners about the importance of personification to the original example. When they talk, I recommend listening to their ideas and providing feedback. Afterward, I suggest asking for volunteers to share insights and writing those points in the third column.

5. Exit Question

This class period concludes with students answering an exit question about why writers use figurative language.

"To conclude today's work on figurative language, you'll write an answer to an exit question. Afterward, I'll ask for two volunteers to share; I'll then collect everyone's answers. The exit question is 'Why would writers use figurative language in their work?'"

I suggest displaying this question while students write their answers. After you collect students' answers, I recommend examining their responses to evaluate their understandings of figurative language. This assessment can inform your upcoming instruction.

Day Two
1. Introduction
You'll begin the second day of work on figurative language by explaining how students' work that day will build on the previous one, sharing the day's key questions, and presenting the agenda.

"Great work yesterday on figurative language! You learned what figurative language is, explored three types of figurative language: similes, metaphors, and personification, thought about its importance to strong writing, examined published examples of it, discussed those examples, and answered an exit question about why writers would use figurative language in their work. Today, we'll explore figurative language even more. We'll review key information about figurative language, apply figurative language to our writing, reflect on its importance to our work, and conclude with an exit question about why figurative language is an important tool for strong writing. Our key questions for today are:

- How can we apply figurative language to our writing?
- Why is figurative language important to the effectiveness of the passages we write?

Today's agenda is:

- Figurative language review
- Writing activity
- Reflection
- Exit question"

I suggest displaying these questions and agenda items while reading them aloud.

2. Figurative Language Review
Next, you'll review key points from the previous day's work on figurative language.

"We'll review important information about figurative language we discussed yesterday. We'll look at a chart that reviews what figurative language is, identifies the types of it that we discussed, describes the importance of figurative language to strong writing, and provides published examples of figurative language."

What Is Figurative Language?	Why Are Some Types of Figurative Language?	Why Is Figurative Language Important to Strong Writing?	What Are Some Published Examples of Figurative Language?
Figurative language is language that is not meant to be understood literally and provides description, emphasis, or expression to a piece of writing.	Some types of figurative language are similes, metaphors, and personification.	Figurative language is important to strong writing because it enhances the reader's understanding of what is being described and allows the author or character to express information in a way that is unique and memorable.	Published simile example: "She ran like a kite that had been let loose on a gusty day, gliding across the sky, not stopping until it reached a tree" (Holt, 2023, p. 5). Published metaphor example: "…the ocean is a strong woman…" (Mendez, 2023, p. 9). Published personification example: "The sun shrugs over the edge of the globe…" (Schmidt, 2023, p. 5).

Figure 5.4.7 Figurative Language Review Information

I suggest displaying this chart and reading its contents aloud. If students showed any confusion about figurative language in the previous day's lesson, I recommend using this time to discuss anything that confused them.

3. Writing Activity

Next, students apply the concept of figurative language to their writing by creating a passage that contains either a simile, a metaphor, or an example of personification and identifying the type of figurative language present in the passage.

"Let's now use figurative language in our writing! You'll create a passage containing either a simile, a metaphor, or an example of personification and identify the type of figurative language you used in the passage."

"We'll first look at an example I wrote: 'In this traffic, our car is a snail.' In this sentence, I used a metaphor by saying the car is a snail."

You can use this example or create your own when you teach this lesson.

"You'll now create your own passage that contains figurative language and identify the type of figurative language you used."

While students create their passages, I recommend moving around the classroom to monitor their progress and support their work.

"Good work creating those passages. Let's have two volunteers share their passages and identify the type of figurative language they used in the passage."

When students share the passages they wrote and identify the figurative language they used, I suggest praising strong examples and identifications. I also suggest providing any needed clarification.

4. Reflection

Here, students revisit the passages they created in the writing activity and reflect on the importance of the figure language to the passage.

"We're going to do a reflective activity with the figurative language passages you just created. You'll revisit the passage you wrote and write an answer to this reflection question: 'Why is the figurative language you used important to the passage you wrote?'"

I suggest displaying this question for students.

"I'll share my reflection about my passage. The passage I wrote was 'In this traffic, our car is a snail.' My answer to the reflection question is 'The figurative language I used, which was a metaphor saying the car is a snail, is important to the passage because it allows me to express that the car moved slowly in traffic in a unique and memorable way.'"

If you use this same example, you can share this reflection with students. If you create a different example, you can share a reflection that goes with that example.

"Look back at the passage you created and write an answer to the reflection question 'Why is the figurative language you used important to the passage you wrote?'"

As students write, I circulate the classroom to check on their work, offering support and encouragement.

"We'll now take two volunteers to share their reflections with the class. After that, everyone will turn in their passages and reflections."

When volunteers share, I recommend praising strong insights and providing any needed clarification.

5. Exit Question

This sequence ends with an exit question on the importance of figurative language.

"We'll close with an exit question on figurative language. You'll write your answer to the question, two volunteers will share, and I'll collect everyone's work. The exit question is 'Why is figurative language an important tool for strong writing?'"

I recommend displaying the exit question. When students answer, I compliment strong work and share additional explanations when needed.

Differentiation Suggestions

This lesson can differentiated in numerous ways:

- Students can work with additional figurative language mentor texts so they can see additional examples of figurative language.
- Students can read figurative language mentor texts on a range of reading levels so they can engage with texts that best fit them.
- Students can create multiple written passages that contain figurative language.
- Students can use a different type of figurative language in each passage they write.

Assessment

I recommend assessing students' knowledge of figurative language and their work in this instructional process in two ways:

- Students' exit question responses.
  - The responses students submit to the two exit questions in this instructional process can help teachers assess their understandings of figurative language. When evaluating students' answers to the day-one exit question, 'Why would writers use figurative language in their work?.' I suggest assessing how well students explain that writers use figurative language to provide description, emphasis, or expression to a piece of writing. When assessing students' responses to the day-two exit question, 'Why is figurative language an important tool for strong writing?,' I recommend evaluating if students are able to explain that figurative language is important to strong writing because it enhances the reader's understanding of what is being described and allows the author or character to express information in a way that is unique and memorable.
- Students' written passages and corresponding reflections.
  - The written passages students create that use figurative language, and their accompanying reflections are also great ways

to assess students' knowledge of figurative language. When assessing students' written passages, I evaluate if they used figurative language in the work, if they correctly identified the figurative language, and if the figurative language makes sense for the passage. When evaluating students' written reflections, I assess the level of insight, clarity, and detail present in their explanations about the importance of the figurative language they used in the passage they created.

Notes

- What worked when teaching this lesson?

- What might you adapt or change the next time you teach it?

References

Holt, K.W. (2023). *The hurricane girls*. Christy Ottaviano Books.
Mendez, J. (2023). *Aniana del Mar jumps in*. Dial Books for Young Readers.
Schmidt, G.D. (2023). *The labors of Hercules Beal*. Clarion Books.

LESSON 5.5

Toward Clarity

Using Commas for Clarity

Overview

This lesson addresses how to use commas to maximize the clarity of a piece of writing. It specifically focuses on three types of comma use: using commas to separate items in a series of three or more, using commas to separate an introductory element from the rest of a sentence, and using commas to show direct address. The lesson spans two class periods. On day one, students will learn about types of comma usage addressed in the lesson, examine examples of them, explore how published writers use these concepts, and consider their impact on a piece of writing. On day two, students will review key ideas about using commas for clarity in writing, apply one of these forms of comma use to their own works, and reflect on the significance of doing so. The instructional process concludes with students answering an exit question about why the comma-use concepts discussed in this lesson sequence are important to strong writing.

Objectives

- Students will understand how commas can be used to maximize the clarity of a piece of writing, with a focus on these comma-use concepts: using commas to separate items in a series of three or more, using commas to separate an introductory element from the rest of a sentence, and using commas to show direct address.

DOI: 10.4324/9781003610656-19

- Students will understand the importance of the comma-use concepts discussed in the lesson.
- Students will be able to apply the comma-use concepts discussed in the lesson to their writing and reflect on the significance of doing so.

Time Frame

Two class periods.

Background Knowledge Required

Students should be familiar with the concept of commas.

Materials Needed

- Figures 5.5.1–5.5.6. They are available in the lesson plan, in Appendix B: Reproducible Graphic Organizers, and electronically on the book's website.
- A board, projector, or piece of chart paper for displaying information.
- Paper for students' writing.

Detailed Plan

Day One
1. Introduction

You'll introduce this lesson sequence by letting students know that they'll be studying the topic of using commas to maximize the clarity of a piece of writing, identifying the types of comma use discussed in the lesson, sharing the day's key questions, and providing the agenda.

"We're going to learn about how writers use commas to make a piece of writing as clear as possible. We'll focus on three types of comma use: using commas to separate items in a series of three or more, using commas to separate an introductory element from the rest of a sentence, and using commas to show direct address. The key questions for today's work are:

- How can commas be used to make a piece of writing as clear as possible?
- What are the characteristics of these comma-use concepts: using commas to separate items in a series of three or more, using commas

to separate an introductory element from the rest of a sentence, and using commas to indicate direct address?
- Why are these comma-use concepts important to strong writing?

Today's agenda is:

- Mini-lesson on using commas for clarity.
- Mentor text examples
- Mentor text discussion and analysis activities
- Exit question"

I recommend displaying these questions and agenda items while reading them aloud.

2. Mini-Lesson on Using Commas for Clarity

You'll teach a mini-lesson on key information regarding using commas for clarity. To do so, you'll explain the topic of using commas for clarity, discuss the types of comma usage addressed in the lesson, and describe the importance of this concept.

"In this mini-lesson, I'll share key ideas about how writers use commas to make a piece of writing as clear as possible. This will be the starting point for our work on this topic. Commas can make writing clear by separating pieces of information and showing the reader that one part of a sentence is set apart from another. We're going to focus on three ways that commas can help make a sentence clear: using commas to separate items in a series of three or more, using commas to separate an introductory element from the rest of the sentence, and using commas to show direct address. Let's look at a chart that describes these three types of comma use."

Type of Comma Use	Description	Example
Using commas to separate items in a series of three or more	Writers use commas to separate the items in a list when listing a series of three or more elements Note: The comma that comes before the word "and" in a series and before the final item in the series is optional unless otherwise stated by a specific writing style guide. I recommend using it for clarity and consistency. This comma is often called the serial comma or Oxford comma.	She loves basketball, hockey, and softball.

Figure 5.5.1 Comma Use Information

(Continued)

Type of Comma Use	Description	Example
Using commas to separate an introductory element from the rest of a sentence	Writers use commas to separate introductory elements from the rest of the sentence. An introductory element begins the sentence and provides background information or context but is not necessary for the sentence to function.	Because the weather is windy and rainy, we moved the party indoors.
Using commas to show direct address	Writers use commas to show someone is being directly addressed. The name or title of whoever is directly addressed is set off by a comma.	Newton, you are a wonderful dog.

Figure 5.5.1 (Continued)

I recommend displaying this chart and reading it aloud while students follow along.

"Now that we've explored these examples of comma usage, let's look at a chart that shares key ideas about using commas for clarity."

Grammatical Concept	What Does It Mean?	What Are Some Types of It?	Why Is It Important to Strong Writing?
Using commas to make a piece of writing as clear as possible	Commas can make writing clear by separating pieces of information and showing the reader that one part of a sentence is set apart from another.	Some ways writers can use commas to make writing clear are: Using commas to separate items in a series of three or more Using commas to separate an introductory element from the rest of a sentence Using commas to show direct address	This grammatical concept is important to strong writing because it helps readers clearly understand the information in a piece of writing. If writers did not use commas to separate information, readers could be confused or could misunderstand the piece.

Figure 5.5.2 Information About Using Commas for Clarity

I suggest displaying this chart and reading its information aloud.

3. Mentor Text Examples

Here, you'll share with students published examples of each of the types of comma use discussed in this lesson. This lets students see how these concepts are used in authentic writing.

"Let's look at published mentor text examples of each of the three types of comma use discussed in the mini-lesson. We'll look at a chart containing these examples."

Mentor Text: Using Commas to Separate Items in a Series of Three or More	**Mentor Text: Using Commas to Separate an Introductory Element from the Rest of a Sentence**	**Mentor Text: Using Commas to Show Direct Address**
"Mr. Hindley was manager, owner, and staff" (Kelly, 2020, p. 2). From *We Dream of Space* by Erin Entrada Kelly	"While I was searching, I found a headband I used to wear all the time when I was younger" (Patrick, 2020, p. 12). From *Tornado Brain* by Cat Patrick	"You gotta *fling* it, Genie" (Reynolds, 2017, p. 3). From *As Brave As You* by Jason Reynolds

Figure 5.5.3 Mentor Texts—Using Commas for Clarity

I recommend displaying these examples and reading them out loud while students follow along. While reading each example, I like to identify the comma or commas in each example that represents the relevant comma-use concept. For example, when discussing the commas that separate items in a series of three or more elements, I like to point out the commas the author uses for that purpose.

4. Mentor Text Discussion and Analysis Activities

Next, you'll help students discuss and analyze the importance of the comma-use concepts to the mentor texts they encountered in the previous activity.

"We'll now think about the importance of the comma use in each of our mentor text examples. We'll look at each of our comma-use mentor texts compared with a revised version that does not use the same comma-use concept. After we examine each example, you'll talk with a partner about a reflection question that asks why you think the comma usage is important to the original text. Let's start with our mentor text for using commas to separate items in a series of three or more."

Original Text	Text Rewritten Without Commas That Separate Items in a Series of Three or More	Reflection Question: Why Are the Commas That Separate Items in the Series Important to the Original Example?
"Mr. Hindley was manager, owner, and staff" (Kelly, 2020, p. 2).	Mr. Hindley was manager owner and staff.	

Figure 5.5.4 Analysis—Using Commas to Separate Items in a Series of Three or More

I recommend displaying this chart, pointing out the differences between the original mentor text and the revised version, and asking students to talk with partners about the reflection question. I then ask for volunteers to share ideas and write highlights from those responses on the chart.

"Let's now think about our mentor text for using commas to separate an introductory element from the rest of a sentence. I'll display a chart containing the original mentor text, a revised version without the comma that separates the introductory element from the rest of the sentence, and a reflection question that asks why the comma that separates the introductory element from the rest of the sentence is important to the original example. After we read the information on the chart, you'll discuss the reflection question with a partner."

Original Text	Text Rewritten Without the Comma That Separates the Introductory Element from the Rest of the Sentence	Reflection Question: Why Is the Comma That Separates the Introductory Element from the Rest of the Sentence Important to the Original Example?
"While I was searching, I found a headband I used to wear all the time when I was younger" (Patrick, 2020, p. 12).	While I was searching I found a headband I used to wear all the time when I was younger.	

Figure 5.5.5 Analysis—Using Commas to Separate an Introductory Element from the Rest of a Sentence

I suggest displaying this chart, noting the difference between the original mentor text and the revised example, and asking students to discuss the reflection question with partners. I then ask for volunteers to share insights and record points from those responses on the chart.

"We'll focus now on our mentor text for using commas to show direct address. I'll share a chart that contains the original mentor text, that text rewritten without the comma that shows direct address, and a reflection question that asks why the comma that shows direct address is important to the original example. We'll look at the information, and then you'll discuss the reflection question with a partner."

Original Text	Text Rewritten Without the Comma That Shows Direct Address	Reflection Question: Why Is the Comma That Shows Direct Address Important to the Original Example?
"You gotta *fling* it, Genie" (Reynolds, 2017, p. 3).	You gotta *fling* it Genie.	

Figure 5.5.6 Analysis—Using Commas to Show Direct Address

I like to display this chart and call attention to the difference between the original mentor text and the revised example before asking students to discuss the reflection question with partners. I recommend then asking volunteers to share ideas and recording information they share on the chart.

5. Exit Question

To conclude this class period, students answer an exit question about why writers use the comma-related concepts discussed in the day's class.

"We'll conclude today's work on comma usage with an exit question. You'll write an answer to the question, and I'll ask for two volunteers to share. Afterward, I'll collect everyone's answers. The exit question is 'Why do writers use the comma-related concepts we discussed today in their writing?'"

I recommend displaying the exit question while reading it aloud. After collecting students' answers, I like to examine their responses to assess their understandings of the comma-related concepts discussed that day.

Day Two
1. Introduction
You'll begin the second day of work on using commas to maximize the clarity of a piece of writing by explaining how the day's activities will build on what

students did previously, presenting the day's key questions, and providing the day's agenda.

"Great job working on comma use yesterday! In yesterday's class, we discussed how writers use commas to make writing as clear as possible. We focused on three types of comma use: using commas to separate items in a series of three or more, using commas to separate an introductory element from the rest of a sentence, and using commas to show direct address. Today, we'll explore these comma-use concepts even further. We'll review key information about using commas to make writing clear, apply this topic to our writing, reflect on its importance, and end with an exit question about the comma-use concepts we're discussing are important to strong writing. Today's key questions are:

- How can we apply the idea of using commas for clarity to our writing?
- Why is the use of commas for clarity important to the effectiveness of our writing?

Today's agenda is:

- Review of using commas for clarity
- Writing activity
- Reflection
- Exit question"

I recommend displaying these questions and agenda items while reading them.

2. Review of Using Commas for Clarity

Here, you'll review key information from the previous day's work about using commas for clarity.

"Let's review important information we discussed yesterday about using commas to make writing as clear as possible. First, let's look again at the chart we saw yesterday that describes three ways that commas can help make a sentence clear: using commas to separate items in a series of three or more, using commas to separate an introductory element from the rest of the sentence, and using commas to show direct address."

At this point in the lesson, you'll display Figure 5.5.1: Comma Use Information, and review each of the types of comma use discussed the previous day. If students showed any confusion about this information in the previous day's class, this is a good time to review those ideas.

"Now, let's review the chart we examined in yesterday's class that explains key points about the concept of commas for clarity."

Here, you'll display Figure 5.5.2: Information About Using Commas for Clarity and read its contents aloud. This is another good time to review any information that was challenging for students in the previous class.

3. Writing Activity

Students now apply the idea of using commas to make writing as clear as possible to their own works by using one of the types of comma use discussed in this lesson to their own writing and identifying the type of comma use they incorporated.

"We'll now apply the ideas of using commas to make writing as clear as possible to our own writing! You'll create a sentence that uses one of the three ways we've discussed that commas can help make a sentence clear: using commas to separate items in a series of three or more, using commas to separate an introductory element from the rest of the sentence, and using commas to show direct address. After you write the sentence, you'll identify the comma-use concept you used in your sentence."

"I'll share an example I wrote: 'Sam, great job on your presentation.' In this sentence, I used a comma after 'Sam' to indicate direct address."

You can use this example or create your own when teaching this lesson.

"Now, you'll write your own sentence that uses one of the three types of comma use we've discussed, and you'll identify the comma-use concept in the sentence."

When students create their sentences, I suggest circulating the classroom and providing feedback on their work.

"Great job creating those sentences. I'll ask for two volunteers to read their sentences and identify the comma-use concept in the sentence."

As students share their sentences and identifications, I recommend praising strong work and providing clarification when needed.

4. Reflection

Next, students revisit the pieces they created in the writing activity and reflect on the importance of the comma-use concept they used in the sentences they wrote.

"We'll now do a reflective activity with the sentences you wrote. You'll reread the sentence you created and write an answer to the reflection question 'Why is the comma-use concept that you used important to the effectiveness of the sentence you wrote?'"

I recommend displaying this question.

"I'll share the reflection I wrote about my sentence 'Sam, great job on your presentation.' My answer to the reflection question is 'In my sentence, I used a comma to indicate direct address. That comma-use concept is important to the effectiveness of the sentence because it clearly shows that I am addressing Sam and separates Sam's name from the rest of the sentence. If I didn't use that comma, it wouldn't be as clear to readers that I'm talking directly to Sam. Sam's name wouldn't be separated from the rest of the sentence like it is now.'"

You can use this same reflection if you share the same example with students. If you create a different example, you'll share a reflection aligned with it.

"Reread the sentence you created and write an answer to the exit question 'Why is the comma-use concept that you used important to the effectiveness of the sentence you wrote?'"

While students write, I move around the classroom to monitor and support their work.

"Let's have two volunteers share their reflections out loud. Then, everyone will turn in their written sentences and reflections."

When students share, I suggest complimenting strong ideas and clarifying any areas of confusion.

5. Exit Question

This lesson sequence ends with an exit question on the importance of the comma-use concepts discussed in this instructional process to strong writing.

"We'll conclude our work on using commas to make writing as clear as possible with an exit question. You'll write an answer to the question, two volunteers will share, and I'll collect everyone's answers. The exit question is 'Why are the comma-related concepts we've discussed yesterday and today important to strong writing?'"

I suggest displaying this question. When volunteers respond, I praise strong insights and provide any needed explanation.

Differentiation Suggestions

This lesson has several differentiation options:

- ◆ Students can work with comma-use concept mentor texts on a range of reading levels so they can read examples that are good fits for them.
- ◆ Students can create additional written passages that contain the comma-use concepts featured in this instructional process.
- ◆ Students can use different comma-use concepts in each of their written passages.

Assessment

I recommend assessing students' knowledge of using commas to maximize the clarity of a piece of writing in two ways:

- ◆ Students' exit question responses.
  - Students' answers to the two exit questions in this instructional process provide important insight into their knowledge of how commas can be used to make writing as clear as possible. When assessing students' responses to the day-one exit question, "Why do writers use the comma-related concepts we discussed today in their writing?," I evaluate how well they explain that writers use these concepts to separate pieces of information and show readers that one part of the sentence is set apart from another. When evaluating students' answers to the day-two exit question, "Why are the comma-related concepts we've discussed yesterday and today important to strong writing?," I assess if students are able to explain that these concepts are important to strong writing because they help readers clearly understand the information in a piece of writing.
- ◆ Students' written examples and corresponding reflections.
  - The written examples students create that use one of the comma concepts addressed in the lesson, and their corresponding reflections are useful for assessing their knowledge of the ideas addressed in this lesson. When evaluating students' written examples, I look to see if they used one of the comma concepts discussed in the lesson in their writing, if they used it correctly, and if they accurately identified it. When assessing students' written reflections, I evaluate the insight and detail present in their statement about the importance of the comma-use concept they used to the effectiveness of their work.

Notes
- ◆ What worked when teaching this lesson?

◆ What might you adapt or change the next time you teach it?

References

Kelly, E.E. (2020). *We dream of space*. Greenwillow Books.
Patrick, C. (2020). *Tornado brain*. Nancy Paulsen Books.
Reynolds, J. (2017). *As brave as you*. Atheneum Books for Young Readers.

SECTION FOUR

Final Thoughts and Resources

Conclusion

Putting Mentor Text-Based Grammar Instruction Into Action in Grades Three to Five

By using the lesson plans in this book, you'll be able to help your elementary school readers and writers think about grammar in engaging and thoughtful ways. Think back to the opening information paragraph of this book's introduction, in which I exclaim, "When I plan lessons on elementary school grammar instruction, I dive into books!" In that paragraph, I highlight the approach that you've seen present in all the lessons featured in this book: the use of outstanding children's and middle-grade literature is central to effective grammar instruction in the elementary school classroom. With this book at your side, you'll be able to use outstanding mentor texts to help your students learn about grammatical concepts in meaningful ways.

In this concluding chapter, I identify four key suggestions for putting the mentor text-based approach to grammar instruction described in this book into action:

- Present grammatical concepts as tools for communication.
- Help students feel empowered by mentor texts.
- Emphasize application and reflection.
- Incorporate your students' needs.

Let's look at each of these suggestions in detail!

Present Grammatical Concepts as Tools for Communication

When our elementary school readers and writers study grammatical concepts, I believe it is especially important to present those concepts as tools for communication. This helps students see the usefulness of the grammatical concepts they'll explore in the lessons discussed in this book. Presenting grammatical concepts as useful tools that are used in communication and expression helps students see these concepts as more than just terms and definitions to memorize. Instead, this instructional approach emphasizes that students are learning about what specific grammatical concepts are so that they can use them in meaningful ways in their own communication. When talking with students about the features of the grammatical concepts in this book's lessons, I like to discuss what the concept is, identify examples of it, and describe why it is important to strong writing. By thinking about each grammatical concept as a tool for strong writing and meaningful communication, students can begin to consider the impact and usefulness of grammar. This approach is especially important to take with our elementary school students as they build the literacy foundations they will use in years to come.

Help Students Feel Empowered by Mentor Texts

The experience of using mentor texts can be an empowering one for students: it allows students to examine the strategies that published authors use and then incorporate those same concepts in their own works. As you teach the lessons in this book, I encourage you to emphasize to students that they are using the same tactics in their writing that published authors use in theirs. By approaching grammar instruction in this way, we can help our students see themselves as writers and feel a connection to the published authors they enjoy. I like to compare the experience of using the same grammatical concept a published writer uses to practicing the same maneuvers as their favorite athlete. For instance, a student who practices using prepositional phrases to add detail like their favorite writer does is taking a similar approach to practicing the same dribbling and shooting skills used by their favorite basketball player. By emphasizing the connection between students' writing and published authors, we can help them feel valued and recognized as writers.

Emphasize Application and Reflection

Another important component of the lesson plans in this book is students' applications of the focal grammatical concepts and their corresponding reflections. In each lesson, you'll support students as they apply the lesson's concept and then help them consider why the concept is important to the piece they created. These activities are designed to help students develop a deep awareness of the significance of the grammatical concepts they learn about. I like to tell students that by using grammatical concepts and reflecting on the impact of those concepts on their work, they'll gain an awareness of how those concepts can impact their writing. I then explain that once students are aware of the importance of those concepts, they'll be able to use them again in meaningful ways. For example, when students develop an in-depth understanding of the impact of relative clauses and the ways they can add detail and description to a piece of writing, they can then use that concept in purposeful ways in their future work.

Incorporate Your Students' Needs

There are numerous ways to align the lessons in this book to your students' needs and incorporate those needs in your implementation of these lessons. For example, I encourage you to take advantage of the differentiation options included in each lesson to align the lesson's content, features, and activities to your class. Another way to align the book's lessons to your specific class relates to the scope and sequence of the lessons. You can sequence the lessons just as they are in this book, or you can make adaptations based on the needs of your students. If you teach fourth grade, for example, you could teach some lessons from the third-grade section to help your students develop strong foundations in those areas, you could teach some lessons from the fifth-grade section that you feel your students are ready to learn, or you could select lessons from all sections that you feel align with your students' abilities and needs. In addition, the lessons in this book can be incorporated into the instructional day in a range of ways based on your students' needs and your available instructional time. Each lesson could take an entire literacy block, but it can also take a part of that if you feel like students would not need the entire block. Also, Appendix C: Lesson Plan Template is another great way to adapt the instructional approach in this book to your students' needs: you can use this planning template with your own mentor texts and examples.

I'm honored that you have chosen this book in your elementary-school grammar instruction. These lessons combine research and practice in ways that are designed to help students in grades three through five grow as readers, writers, and thinkers. The plans and activities in this text are designed to engage students, empower them, and help them develop meaningful understandings of grammar. They are structured to deepen students' awareness of what grammatical concepts are, why they're important to strong writing, how to use them in their works, and why doing so is important to the effectiveness of their writing. Thank you for choosing to use these lessons in your classroom!

Appendix A
Annotated Bibliography of Mentor Texts

This annotated bibliography is designed to provide you with a quick reference guide to all of the mentor text examples used in this book. If you want to find one of the book's mentor text examples quickly, you can use this guide to find all of the published excerpts featured in the book. The guide is organized alphabetically by author's last name, and each entry includes important details designed to help you use literature to teach these grammatical concepts. It contains the following information: the titles and authors of the works of literature featured in this book, a key grammatical concept found in each work, and an excerpt from that work, previously featured in the book, that demonstrates exactly how the author uses that grammatical concept.

Beatty, R. (2015). *Serafina and the black cloak.* Disney Hyperion.
Book Title: *Serafina and the Black Cloak*
Author: Robert Beatty
Key Grammatical Concept: Capitalization
Excerpt: "She crept forward along the wall" (p. 4)

Booth, C. (2014). *Kinda like brothers.* Scholastic.
Book Title: *Kinda Like Brothers*
Author: Coe Booth
Key Grammatical Concept: Coordinating conjunction
Excerpt: "It was still the middle of the night, and I probably hadn't even been asleep for more than an hour" (p. 2).

Cervantes, A. (2019). *Me, Frida, and the secret of the peacock ring.* Scholastic.
Book Title: *Me, Frida, and the Secret of the Peacock Ring*
Author: Angela Cervantes
Key Grammatical Concept: Strong verb
Excerpt: "Paloma glanced at the black cat and monkey in the painting" (p. 10).

Chapman, E. (2023). *The scroll of chaos*. Scholastic.
Book Title: *The Scroll of Chaos*
Author: Elsie Chapman
Key Grammatical Concept: Adverb
Excerpt: "As Libby Pearson (my best friend) puts away her violin beside me, she clumsily bangs the instrument against the leg of her chair" (p. 1).

Elliott, Z. (2018). *Dragons in a bag*. Yearling.
Book Title: *Dragons in a Bag*
Author: Zetta Elliott
Key Grammatical Concept: Subject-verb agreement
Excerpt: "She speaks slowly and politely" (p. 2).

Franklin, M.S. (2015). *Extraordinary*. Sky Pony Press.
Book Title: *Extraordinary*
Author: Miriam Spitzer Franklin
Key Grammatical Concept: Capitalization
Excerpt: "Anna and I dressed up as salt and pepper shakers for Halloween" (p. 2).

Getten, K. (2020). *When life gives you mangos*. Yearling.
Book Title: *When Life Gives You Mangos*
Author: Kereen Getten
Key Grammatical Concept: Prepositional phrase
Excerpt: "I have a secret hideout behind the house" (p. 8).

Gibbs, S. (2023). *Spy school goes north*. Simon & Schuster Books for Young Readers.
Book Title: *Spy School Goes North*
Author: Stuart Gibbs
Key Grammatical Concept: Subject-verb agreement
Excerpt: "At the top of the cliff, Zoe sniffed the air" (p. 5).

Gidwitz, A. (2018). *The creature of the pines*. Dutton Children's Books.
Book Title: *The Creature of the Pines*
Author: Adam Gidwitz
Key Grammatical Concept: Adjective
Excerpt: "Elliot Eisner stood at the front of the bus, looking down the long aisle" (p. 1).

Copyright material from Sean Ruday (2026), *Teaching Elementary Grammar with Mentor Texts*, Routledge

Holt, K.W. (2023). *The hurricane girls.* Christy Ottaviano Books.
Book Title: *The Hurricane Girls*
Author: Kimberly Willis Holt
Key Grammatical Concept: Figurative Language: Simile
Excerpt: "She ran like a kite that had been let loose on a gusty day, gliding across the sky, not stopping until it reached a tree" (p. 5).

Johnson, V. (2018). *The Parker inheritance.* Scholastic.
Book Title: *The Parker Inheritance*
Author: Varian Johnson
Key Grammatical Concept: Capitalization
Excerpt: "You should give Cousin Lucretia a ring" (p. 42).

Kadohata, C. *The thing about luck.* Atheneum Books for Young Readers.
Book Title: *The Thing About Luck*
Author: Cynthia Kadohata
Key Grammatical Concept: Specific noun
Excerpt: "This infected mosquito might bite you" (p. 2).

Keller, T. (2020). *When you trap a tiger.* Yearling.
Book Title: *When You Trap a Tiger*
Author: Tae Keller
Key Grammatical Concept: Coordinating conjunction
Excerpt: "My voice catches in my throat, and I stumble over my words" (p. 6).

Kelly, E.E. (2017). *Hello, universe.* Greenwillow Books.
Book Title: *Hello, Universe*
Author: Erin Entrada Kelly
Key Grammatical Concept: Using commas and quotation marks when writing dialogue
Excerpt: "You know," she began, "I had a dream about the Stone Boy again last night" (p. 5)

Kelly, E.E. (2020). *We dream of space.* Greenwillow Books.
Book Title: *We Dream of Space*
Author: Erin Entrada Kelly
Key Grammatical Concept: Using commas for clarity
Excerpt: "Mr. Hindley was manager, owner, and staff" (p. 2).

Copyright material from Sean Ruday (2026), *Teaching Elementary Grammar with Mentor Texts*, Routledge

Kelly, L. (2019). *Song for a whale.* Yearling.
Book Title: *Song for a Whale*
Author: Lynne Kelly
Key Grammatical Concept: Using commas and quotation marks when writing dialogue
Excerpt: He looked at Grandma and said, "Iris has gotten used to her school" (p. 51).

Krishnaswami, U. (2017). *Step up to the plate, Maria Singh.* Lee & Low Books.
Book Title: *Step Up to the Plate, Maria Singh*
Author: Uma Krishnaswami
Key Grammatical Concept: Modal auxiliary
Excerpt: "There will be other girls' teams in the county" (p. 17).

Marks, J. (2020). *From the desk of Zoe Washington.* Katherine Tegen Books.
Book Title: *From the Desk of Zoe Washington*
Author: Janae Marks
Key Grammatical Concept: Subordinating conjunction
Excerpt: "Since my mom and stepdad thought it was gross, we usually only got those toppings on half a pie" (p. 5).

Medina, M. (2018). *Merci Suárez changes gears.* Candlewick Press.
Book Title: *Merci Suárez Changes Gears*
Author: Meg Medina
Key Grammatical Concept: Correlative conjunctions
Excerpt: "You either like someone or you don't" (p. 126).

Mendez, J. (2023). *Aniana del Mar jumps in.* Dial Books for Young Readers.
Book Title: *Aniana del Mar Jumps in*
Author: Jasminne Mendez
Key Grammatical Concept: Figurative Language: Metaphor
Excerpt: "…the ocean is a strong woman…" (p. 9).

O'Connor, B. (2016). *Wish.* Farrar Straus Giroux.
Book Title: *Wish*
Author: Barbara O'Connor
Key Grammatical Concept: Capitalization
Excerpt: "Not even a Chinese restaurant" (p. 6).

Copyright material from Sean Ruday (2026), *Teaching Elementary Grammar with Mentor Texts*, Routledge

Patrick, C. (2020). *Tornado brain*. Nancy Paulsen Books.
Book Title: *Tornado Brain*
Author: Cat Patrick
Key Grammatical Concept: Using commas for clarity
Excerpt: "While I was searching, I found a headband I used to wear all the time when I was younger" (p. 12).

Pennypacker, S. (2016). *Pax*. Balzer + Bray.
Book Title: *Pax*
Author: Sara Pennypacker
Key Grammatical Concept: Using commas and quotation marks when writing dialogue
Excerpt: "Can I have it?" (p. 9).

Raúf, O.Q. (2018). *The boy at the back of the class*. Yearling.
Book Title: *The Boy at the Back of the Class*
Author: Onjali Q. Raúf
Key Grammatical Concept: Using commas and quotation marks when writing dialogue
Excerpt: "He's probably left already," said Josie (p. 17).

Reed, D. (2021). *Simon B. Rhymin'*. Little, Brown and Company.
Book Title: *Simon B. Rhymin'*
Author: Dwayne Reed
Key Grammatical Concept: Subject-verb agreement
Excerpt: "He was so excited!" (p. 5).

Reynolds, J. (2017). *As brave as you*. Atheneum Books for Young Readers.
Book Title: *As Brave as You*
Author: Jason Reynolds
Key Grammatical Concept: Using commas for clarity
Excerpt: "You gotta *fling* it, Genie" (p. 3).

Rhodes, J.P. (2016). *Bayou magic*. Little, Brown Books for Young Readers.
Book Title: *Bayou Magic*
Author: Jewell Parker Rhodes
Key Grammatical Concept: Relative clause
Excerpt: "I rub my cheek, which is creased from the ridges on the seat" (p. 12).

Copyright material from Sean Ruday (2026), *Teaching Elementary Grammar with Mentor Texts*, Routledge

Schmidt, G.D. (2023). *The labors of Hercules Beal.* Clarion Books.
Book Title: *The Labors of Hercules Beal*
Author: Gary D. Schmidt
Key Grammatical Concept: Figurative Language: Personification
Excerpt: "The sun shrugs over the edge of the globe…" (p. 5).

Soontornvat, C. (2022). *The last mapmaker.* Candlewick Press.
Book Title: *The Last Mapmaker*
Author: Christina Soontornvat
Key Grammatical Concept: Complex sentence
Excerpt: "If they knew the truth, they would think I was nothing" (p. 7).

Thomas, A. (2023). *Nic Blake and The Remarkables: The Manifestor Prophecy.* Balzer + Bray.
Book Title: *Nic Blake and The Remarkables: The Manifestor Prophecy*
Author: Angie Thomas
Key Grammatical Concept: Capitalization
Excerpt: "Dad and I jump" (p. 4).

Wan-Long Shang, W. (2015). *The way home looks now.* Scholastic.
Book Title: *The Way Home Looks Now*
Author: Wendy Wan-Long Shang
Key Grammatical Concept: Pronoun-antecedent agreement
Excerpt: "I watched him fold his jean jacket and put it in his duffel bag" (p. 35).

Weeks, S., & Varadarajan, G. (2016). *Save me a seat.* Scholastic.
Book Title: *Save Me a Seat*
Author: Sarah Weeks and Gita Varadarajan
Key Grammatical Concept: Compound Sentence
Excerpt: "This is my first day of school in America, and things are not going well" (p. 7).

Williams-Garcia, R. (2013). *P.S. Be eleven.* HarperCollins.
Book Title: *P.S. Be Eleven*
Author: Rita Williams-Garcia
Key Grammatical Concept: Capitalization
Excerpt: "We held hands and leaned to the left to watch New York come in closer" (p. 2).

Copyright material from Sean Ruday (2026), *Teaching Elementary Grammar with Mentor Texts*, Routledge

Winston, S. (2023). *The braid girls*. Little, Brown and Company.
Book Title: *The Braid Girls*
Author: Sherri Winston
Key Grammatical Concept: Interjection
Excerpt: "*Sweet!* That's when my braces come off!" (p. 6).

Yang, K. (2018). *Front desk*. Scholastic.
Book Title: *Front Desk*
Author: Kelly Yang
Key Grammatical Concept: Prepositional phrase
Excerpt: "I counted the keys in my hand" (p. 29).

Yee, L. (2022). *Maizy Chen's last chance*. Random House Books for Young Readers.
Book Title: *Maizy Chen's Last Chance*
Author: Lisa Yee
Key Grammatical Concept: Simple sentence
Excerpt: "Her family is really close" (p. 1).

Appendix B

Reproducible Graphic Organizers

This resource contains all of the graphic organizers featured in the book's lesson plans. The graphic organizers are grouped by their corresponding lesson plans for clarity and convenient access. These graphic organizers can also be downloaded from the Routledge website.

Graphic Organizers from Lesson 3.1: Let's Agree: Subject-Verb Agreement

Grammatical Concept	What Is Subject-Verb Agreement?	What Are Some Key Ideas to Know About Subject-Verb Agreement?	Why Is Subject-Verb Agreement Important to Strong Writing?
Subject-verb agreement	Subject-verb agreement is the idea that subjects and verbs must match in number: singular subjects go with singular verbs, and plural subjects go with plural verbs.	Not all verbs change based on whether the subject is singular or plural. For example, in the sentence "The goats walked," the verb would be "walked" whether the subject is singular or plural. A situation in which a verb changes based on whether the subject is singular or plural is in third-person narration in the present tense. For instance, the sentence "The goat walks" becomes "The goats walk" if the subject goes from singular to plural.	Subject-verb agreement is important to strong writing because it helps readers clearly understand what the writer is expressing. If there is confusion in subject-verb agreement, readers could be distracted or not correctly understand a statement.

Figure 3.1.1 Subject-Verb Agreement Information

(Continued)

Copyright material from Sean Ruday (2026), *Teaching Elementary Grammar with Mentor Texts*, Routledge

Grammatical Concept	What Is Subject-Verb Agreement?	What Are Some Key Ideas to Know About Subject-Verb Agreement?	Why Is Subject-Verb Agreement Important to Strong Writing?
		The verb also frequently changes based on whether a subject is singular or plural when that verb is a form of "be." For example, the sentence "The goat was outside" uses the singular verb "was" to go with its singular subject. "The goats were outside" uses the plural verb "were" to go with its plural subject.	

Figure 3.1.1 (Continued)

Example One: Verb Does Not Change Based on Whether Subject Is Singular or Plural	Example Two: Third-Person Narration in Present Tense	Example Three: Sentence Containing Form of the Verb "Be"
"At the top of the cliff, Zoe sniffed the air" (Gibbs, 2023, p. 5).	"She speaks slowly and politely" (Elliott, 2019, p. 2).	"He was so excited!" (Reed, 2021, p. 5).

Figure 3.1.2 Subject-Verb Agreement Mentor Text Examples

Copyright material from Sean Ruday (2026), *Teaching Elementary Grammar with Mentor Texts*, Routledge

Original Mentor Text Example	Revised Example That Does Not Contain Subject-Verb Agreement	Why the Subject-Verb Agreement Is Important to the Original Example
"At the top of the cliff, Zoe sniffed the air" (Gibbs, 2023, p. 5).	At the top of the cliff, Zoe and I sniffs the air.	

Figure 3.1.3 Subject-Verb Agreement Discussion Example One: Original Verb Does Not Change Based on Whether Subject Is Singular or Plural

Original Mentor Text Example	Revised Example That Does Not Contain Subject-Verb Agreement	Why the Subject-Verb Agreement Is Important to the Original Example
"She speaks slowly and politely" (Elliott, 2019, p. 2).	She speak slowly and politely.	

Figure 3.1.4 Subject-Verb Agreement Discussion Example Two: Third Person Narration in Present Tense

Original Mentor Text Example	Revised Example That Does Not Contain Subject-Verb Agreement	Why the Subject-Verb Agreement Is Important to the Original Example
"He was so excited!" (Reed, 2021, p. 5).	He and his friend was so excited!	

Figure 3.1.5 Subject-Verb Agreement Discussion Example Three: Sentence Containing Form of the Verb "Be"

Copyright material from Sean Ruday (2026), *Teaching Elementary Grammar with Mentor Texts*, Routledge

What Is Subject-Verb Agreement?	What Are Some Key Ideas to Know About Subject-Verb Agreement?	Why Is Subject-Verb Agreement Important to Strong Writing?	What Are Published Examples of Subject-Verb Agreement?
Subject-verb agreement is the idea that subjects and verbs must match in number: singular subjects go with singular verbs, and plural subjects go with plural verbs.	Not all verbs change based on whether the subject is singular or plural. For example, in the sentence "The goats walked," the verb would be "walked" whether the subject is singular or plural. A situation in which a verb changes based on whether the subject is singular or plural is in third-person narration in the present tense. For instance, the sentence "The goat walks" becomes "The goats walk" if the subject goes from singular to plural. The verb also frequently changes based on whether a subject is singular or plural when that verb is a form of "be." For example, the sentence "The goat was outside" uses the singular	Subject-verb agreement is important to strong writing because it helps readers clearly understand what the writer is expressing. If there is confusion in subject-verb agreement, readers could be distracted or not correctly understand a statement.	Example One: Verb Does Not Change Based on Whether Subject is Singular or Plural: "At the top of the cliff, Zoe sniffed the air" (Gibbs, 2023, p. 5). Third-Person Narration in Present Tense: "She speaks slowly and politely" (Elliott, 2019, p. 2). Sentence Containing Form of the Verb "Be": "He was so excited!" (Reed, 2021, p. 5).

Figure 3.1.6 Subject-Verb Agreement Review Information

(Continued)

What Is Subject-Verb Agreement?	What Are Some Key Ideas to Know About Subject-Verb Agreement?	Why Is Subject-Verb Agreement Important to Strong Writing?	What Are Published Examples of Subject-Verb Agreement?
	verb "was" to go with its singular subject. "The goats were outside" uses the plural verb "were" to go with its plural subject.		

Figure 3.1.6 (Continued)

Graphic Organizers from Lesson 3.2: Descriptive Information: Adjectives

Grammatical Concept	What Are Adjectives?	What Are Some Examples of Adjectives?	What Are Some Ways Adjectives Can Look in Writing?	Why Are Adjectives Important to Strong Writing?
Adjectives	Adjectives are descriptive words that provide information about a noun or pronoun.	Some examples of adjectives are colorful, cute, fun, young, old, hot, cold, beautiful, special, large, small, fast, and happy.	The **happy** fans cheered. We felt the **cold** wind. We saw a **large** elephant at the zoo.	Adjectives are important to strong writing because they help the reader understand the features of the noun or pronoun being described.

Figure 3.2.1 Adjective Information

Copyright material from Sean Ruday (2026), *Teaching Elementary Grammar with Mentor Texts*, Routledge

Original Text	Revised Version With Adjective Removed
"Elliot Eisner stood at the front of the bus, looking down the long aisle" (Gidwitz, 2018, p. 1).	Elliot Eisner stood at the front of the bus, looking down the aisle.

Figure 3.2.2 Original Text vs. Revised Version With Adjective Removed

Reflection Question One	Reflection Question Two
How is the sentence different without the adjective "long"?	Why do you think the author used this adjective in the sentence?

Figure 3.2.3 Adjective Reflection Questions Graphic Organizer

Copyright material from Sean Ruday (2026), *Teaching Elementary Grammar with Mentor Texts*, Routledge

What Are Adjectives?	What Are Some Examples of Adjectives?	Why Are Adjectives Important to Strong Writing?	What Is a Published Example of Adjective Use?
Adjectives are descriptive words that provide information about a noun or pronoun.	Some examples of adjectives are colorful, cute, fun, young, old, hot, cold, beautiful, special, large, small, fast, and happy.	Adjectives are important to strong writing because they help the reader understand the features of the noun or pronoun being described.	"Elliot Eisner stood at the front of the bus, looking down the **long** aisle" (Gidwitz, 2018, p. 1).

Figure 3.2.4 Adjective Review Information

Graphic Organizers from Lesson 3.3: The Power of Explanation: Adverbs

Grammatical Concept	What Are Adverbs?	What Are Some Examples of Adverbs?	What Are Some Ways Adverbs Can Look in Writing?	Why Are Adverbs Important to Strong Writing?
Adverbs	Adverbs are words that describe verbs, adjectives, and other adverbs. They answer questions like "How?," "When?," "Where?," and "To What Extent?"	Some examples of words that can function as adverbs are quickly, slowly, carefully, wildly, extremely, soon, often, frequently, immediately, happily, everywhere, exactly, truly, and very.	The fans **quickly** went to their seats. We walked **carefully** through the woods. I **immediately** recognized you. I searched **everywhere**. We'll see them **soon**. She ran **very** fast.	Adverbs are important to strong writing because the explanation they give can help readers understand what the author is communicating.

Figure 3.3.1 Adverb Information

Original Text	Revised Version With Adverb Removed
"As Libby Pearson (my best friend) puts away her violin beside me, she clumsily bangs the instrument against the leg of her chair" (p. 1).	As Libby Pearson (my best friend) puts away her violin beside me, she bangs the instrument against the leg of her chair.

Figure 3.3.2 Original Text vs. Revised Version With Adverb Removed

Reflection Question One	Reflection Question Two
How is the sentence different without the adverb "clumsily"?	Why do you think the author used this adverb in the sentence?

Figure 3.3.3 Adverb Reflection Questions Graphic Organizer

Copyright material from Sean Ruday (2026), *Teaching Elementary Grammar with Mentor Texts*, Routledge

What Are Adverbs?	What Are Some Examples of Adverbs?	Why Are Adverbs Important to Strong Writing?	What Is a Published Example of Adverb Use?
Adverbs are words that describe verbs, adjectives, and other adverbs. They answer questions like "How?," "When?," "Where?," and "To What Extent?"	Some examples of words that can function as adverbs are quickly, slowly, carefully, wildly, extremely, soon, often, frequently, immediately, happily, everywhere, exactly, truly, and very.	Adverbs are important to strong writing because the explanation they give can help readers understand what the author is communicating.	"As Libby Pearson (my best friend) puts away her violin beside me, she **clumsily** bangs the instrument against the leg of her chair" (Chapman, 2023, p. 1).

Figure 3.3.4 Adverb Review Information

Graphic Organizers from Lesson 3.4: Building Sentences: Simple, Compound, and Complex Sentences

Sentence Type	Description	Example	Importance to Strong Writing
Simple sentence	A simple sentence is made up of one independent clause.	Julie played basketball.	Simple sentences are important to strong writing because they express information directly and clearly.

Figure 3.4.1 Key Information About Simple Sentences

Sentence Type	Description	Examples	Importance to Strong Writing
Compound sentence	A compound sentence is made up of two or more independent clauses joined by a coordinator, such as a comma and coordinating conjunction or a semicolon.	Julie played basketball, and Jeff played soccer. Julie played basketball; Jeff played soccer.	Compound sentences are important to strong writing because they connect ideas and help the flow of a piece of writing.

Figure 3.4.2 Key Information About Compound Sentences

Copyright material from Sean Ruday (2026), *Teaching Elementary Grammar with Mentor Texts*, Routledge

Sentence Type	Description	Example	Importance to Strong Writing
Complex sentences	A complex sentence is made up of an independent clause and at least one dependent clause.	Because she loves the sport, Julie played basketball.	Complex sentences are important to strong writing because the background information and context they provide help the reader understand what's taking place.

Figure 3.4.3 Key Information About Complex Sentences

Published Simple Sentence Example	Published Compound Sentence Example	Published Complex Sentence Example
"Her family is really close" (Yee, 2022, p. 1). From *Maizy Chen's Last Chance* by Lisa Yee	"This is my first day of school in America, and things are not going well" (Weeks & Varadarajan, 2016, p. 7). From *Save Me a Seat* by Sarah Weeks and Gita Varadarajan	"If they knew the truth, they would think I was nothing" (Soontornvat, 2022, p. 7). From *The Last Mapmaker* by Christina Soontornvat

Figure 3.4.4 Published Examples of Simple, Compound, and Complex Sentences

Simple Sentence Mentor Text	Benefits of Using This Sentence Type
"Her family is really close" (Yee, 2022, p. 1).	

Figure 3.4.5 Simple Sentence Benefits Analysis Chart

Copyright material from Sean Ruday (2026), *Teaching Elementary Grammar with Mentor Texts*, Routledge

Compound Sentence Mentor Text	Benefits of Using This Sentence Type
"This is my first day of school in America, and things are not going well" (Weeks & Varadarajan, 2016, p. 7).	

Figure 3.4.6 Compound Sentence Benefits Analysis Chart

Complex Sentence Mentor Text	Benefits of Using This Sentence Type
"If they knew the truth, they would think I was nothing" (Soontornvat, 2022, p. 7).	

Figure 3.4.7 Complex Sentence Benefits Analysis Chart

Copyright material from Sean Ruday (2026), *Teaching Elementary Grammar with Mentor Texts*, Routledge

Sentence Type	Description	Published Example	Importance to Strong Writing
Simple sentence	A simple sentence is made up of one independent clause.	"Her family is really close" (Yee, 2022, p. 1).	Simple sentences are important to strong writing because they express information directly and clearly.
Compound sentence	A compound sentence is made up of two or more independent clauses joined by a coordinator, such as a comma and coordinating conjunction or a semicolon.	"This is my first day of school in America, and things are not going well" (Weeks & Varadarajan, 2016, p. 7).	Compound sentences are important to strong writing because they connect ideas and help the flow of a piece of writing.
Complex sentence	A complex sentence is made up of an independent clause and at least one dependent clause.	"If they knew the truth, they would think I was nothing" (Soontornvat, 2022, p. 7).	Complex sentences are important to strong writing because the background information and context they provide help the reader understand what's taking place.

Figure 3.4.8 Simple, Compound, and Complex Sentence Review Information

Copyright material from Sean Ruday (2026), *Teaching Elementary Grammar with Mentor Texts*, Routledge

Graphic Organizers from Lesson 3.5: In Dialogue: Using Commas and Quotation Marks When Writing Dialogue

Grammatical Concept	What Is It?	Why Is It Important to Strong Writing?	What Are Examples of How It's Used?
Using commas and quotation marks when writing dialogue.	When writing dialogue, writers use the punctuation marks of commas (when needed) and quotation marks to show what a speaker is saying.	This concept is important to strong writing because it allows writers to clearly separate a speaker's words from the rest of the piece.	Example One: The Speaker Tag Comes Before the Quotation: Joe said, "I want to see a manatee." Example Two: The Speaker Tag Follows the Quotation: "I want to see a manatee," Joe said. Example Three: The Speaker Tag Interrupts the Quotation: "I want," Joe said," to see a manatee." Example Four: There Is No Speaker Tag: "I want to see a manatee."

Figure 3.5.1 Information and Examples Regarding Using Commas and Quotation Marks When Writing Dialogue

Example One: The Speaker Tag Comes Before the Quotation	Example Two: The Speaker Tag Follows the Quotation	Example Three: The Speaker Tag Interrupts the Quotation	Example Four: There Is No Speaker Tag
He looked at Grandma and said, "Iris has gotten used to her school" (Kelly, 2019, p. 51).	"He's probably left already," said Josie (Raúf, 2018, p. 17).	"You know," she began, "I had a dream about the Stone Boy again last night" (Kelly, 2017, p. 5).	"Can I have it?" (Pennypacker, 2016, p. 9).

Figure 3.5.2 Published Examples of Sentences That Use Commas (When Needed) and Quotation Marks to Show Dialogue

Mentor Text Example	Example Without Comma and Quotation Marks That Shows Dialogue	Why This Punctuation Is Important to the Sentence
He looked at Grandma and said, "Iris has gotten used to her school" (Kelly, 2019, p. 51).	He looked at Grandma and said Iris has gotten used to her school.	

Figure 3.5.3 Mentor Text Discussion Chart. Example One: The Speaker Tag Comes Before the Quotation

Copyright material from Sean Ruday (2026), *Teaching Elementary Grammar with Mentor Texts*, Routledge

Mentor Text Example	Example Without Comma and Quotation Marks That Shows Dialogue	Why This Punctuation Is Important to the Sentence
"He's probably left already," said Josie (Raúf, 2018, p. 17).	He's probably left already said Josie.	

Figure 3.5.4 Mentor Text Discussion Chart. Example Two: The Speaker Tag Follows the Quotation

Mentor Text Example	Example Without Commas and Quotation Marks That Shows Dialogue	Why This Punctuation Is Important to the Sentence
"You know," she began, "I had a dream about the Stone Boy again last night" (Kelly, 2017, p. 5).	You know she began I had a dream about the Stone Boy again last night.	

Figure 3.5.5 Mentor Text Discussion Chart. Example Three: The Speaker Tag Interrupts the Quotation

Copyright material from Sean Ruday (2026), *Teaching Elementary Grammar with Mentor Texts*, Routledge

Mentor Text Example	Example Without Quotation Marks That Shows Dialogue	Why This Punctuation Is Important to the Sentence
"Can I have it?" (Pennypacker, 2016, p. 9).	Can I have it?	

Figure 3.5.6 Mentor Text Discussion Chart. Example Three: There Is No Speaker Tag

Your Original Passage	Revised Version Without the Commas (If Any) and Quotation Marks That Shows Dialogue	Why the Punctuation You Used to Show Dialogue Is Important to the Sentence

Figure 3.5.7 Reflection Graphic Organizer

Copyright material from Sean Ruday (2026), *Teaching Elementary Grammar with Mentor Texts*, Routledge

Graphic Organizers from Lesson 4.1: A Big Deal: Capitalization

Grammatical Concept	What Is Capitalization?	Why Is Capitalization Important to Strong Writing?
Capitalization	Capitalization is the use of capital, or uppercase letters, when writing.	Capitalization is important to strong writing because it makes writing clear and helps readers understand a piece of writing without being distracted by capitalization mistakes.

Figure 4.1.1 Capitalization Information

Capitalization Rule	Example
Capitalize the first letter of the first word in a sentence.	**We** are going to the party.
Capitalize the pronoun *I*.	**I** am outside.
Capitalize proper nouns.	We traveled to **Boston**.
Capitalize titles that come before names.	They met **Mayor Smith**.
Capitalize days of the week, months of the year, and holidays.	**Thanksgiving** takes place on a **Thursday** in **November**.
Capitalize the names of countries, nationalities, and specific languages.	She likes to visit **Canada**.

Figure 4.1.2 Key Capitalization Rules and Examples

Copyright material from Sean Ruday (2026), *Teaching Elementary Grammar with Mentor Texts*, Routledge

Capitalization Rule	Published Example
Capitalize the first letter of the first word in a sentence.	"**She** crept forward along the wall" (Beatty, 2015, p. 4). From *Serafina and the Black Cloak* by Robert Beatty
Capitalize the pronoun *I*.	"Dad and **I** jump" (Thomas, 2023, p. 4). From *Nic Blake and the Remarkables: The Manifestor Prophecy* by Angie Thomas
Capitalize proper nouns.	"We held hands and leaned to the left to watch **New York** come in closer" (Williams-Garcia, 2013, p. 2). From *P.S. Be Eleven* by Rita Williams-Garcia
Capitalize titles that come before names.	"You should give **Cousin** Lucretia a ring" (Johnson, 2018, p. 42). From *The Parker Inheritance* by Varian Johnson
Capitalize days of the week, months of the year, and holidays.	"Anna and I dressed up as salt and pepper shakers for **Halloween**" (Franklin, 2015, p. 2). From *Extraordinary* by Miriam Spitzer Franklin
Capitalize the names of countries, nationalities, and specific languages.	"Not even a **Chinese** restaurant" (O'Connor, 2016, p. 6). From *Wish* by Barbara O'Connor

Figure 4.1.3 Published Examples of Capitalization Rules

Published Example	Written Without Key Capitalization Rule Used	Why the Capitalization in the Original Example Is Important
"**She** crept forward along the wall" (Beatty, 2015, p. 4). From *Serafina and the Black Cloak* by Robert Beatty	she crept forward along the wall.	
"Dad and **I** jump" (Thomas, 2023, p. 4). From *Nic Blake and the Remarkables: The Manifestor Prophecy* by Angie Thomas	Dad and i jump.	
"We held hands and leaned to the left to watch **New York** come in closer" (Williams-Garcia, 2013, p. 2). From *P.S. Be Eleven* by Rita Williams-Garcia	We held hands and leaned to the left to watch new york come in closer.	
"You should give **Cousin** Lucretia a ring" (Johnson, 2018, p. 42). From *The Parker Inheritance* by Varian Johnson	You should give cousin Lucretia a ring.	
"Anna and I dressed up as salt and pepper shakers for **Halloween**" (Franklin, 2015, p. 2). From *Extraordinary* by Miriam Spitzer Franklin	Anna and I dressed up as salt and pepper shakers for halloween.	
"Not even a **Chinese** restaurant" (O'Connor, 2016, p. 6). From *Wish* by Barbara O'Connor	Not even a chinese restaurant.	

Figure 4.1.4 Mentor Text Comparison and Discussion Chart

Your Original Passage	Rewritten Without the Capitalization Rules You Used	Why the Capitalization in the Original Passage Is Important

Figure 4.1.5 Reflection Graphic Organizer

Graphic Organizers from Lesson 4.2: Showing Conditions: Modal Auxiliaries

Grammatical Concept	What Are Modal Auxiliaries?	What Words Are Used as Modal Auxiliaries?	What Are Some Ways Modal Auxiliaries Can Look in Writing?	Why Are Modal Auxiliaries Important to Strong Writing?
Modal Auxiliaries	Modal auxiliaries are words that give information about the possibility, likelihood, or necessity of something happening.	The following words are used as modal auxiliaries: *will, would, shall, should, can, could, may, might, must,* and *ought to.*	I **must** leave now. You **should** read this book. I **can** go to the movies.	Modal auxiliaries are important to strong writing because writers can use them to show exactly how likely, possible, or necessary something is.

Figure 4.2.1 Modal Auxiliary Information

Original Text	Revised Version With Different Modal Auxiliary
"There will be other girls' teams in the county" (Krishnaswami, 2017, p. 17).	There might be other girls' teams in the county.

Figure 4.2.2 Original Text vs. Revised Version With Different Modal Auxiliary

Copyright material from Sean Ruday (2026), *Teaching Elementary Grammar with Mentor Texts*, Routledge

Reflection Question One	Reflection Question Two
How is the original sentence with the modal auxiliary "will" different from the revised version with the modal auxiliary "might"?	Why is the modal auxiliary "will" important to the original sentence?

Figure 4.2.3 Modal Auxiliary Reflection Questions Graphic Organizer

What Are Modal Auxiliaries?	What Words Are Used as Modal Auxiliaries?	Why Are Modal Auxiliaries Important to Strong Writing?	What Is a Published Example of Modal Auxiliary Use?
Modal auxiliaries are words that give information about the possibility, likelihood, or necessity of something happening.	The following words are used as modal auxiliaries: *will, would, shall, should, can, could, may, might, must,* and *ought to.*	Modal auxiliaries are important to strong writing because writers can use them to show exactly how likely, possible, or necessary something is.	"There **will** be other girls' teams in the county" (Krishnaswami, 2017, p. 17).

Figure 4.2.4 Modal Auxiliary Review Information

Copyright material from Sean Ruday (2026), *Teaching Elementary Grammar with Mentor Texts*, Routledge

Graphic Organizers from Lesson 4.3: Elaborating on Information: Prepositional Phrases

At	During
Above	In
Across	On
Before	Through
Down	Under

Figure 4.3.1 Some Frequently Used Prepositions

Grammatical Concept	What Are Prepositional Phrases?	What Are Examples of Prepositional Phrases?	How Can Prepositional Phrases Look in Writing?	Why Are Prepositional Phrases Important to Strong Writing?
Prepositional phrases	Prepositional phrases are descriptive phrases that begin with a preposition and end with a noun or pronoun called the object of the preposition.	On the chair Above the trees Under the desk Across the field	The cat slept **on the chair.** The birds flew **above the trees.** We looked **under the desk.** She kicked the ball **across the field.**	Prepositional phrases are important to strong writing because of the detail and description they add. This information can give the reader a clear understanding of what's being discussed.

Figure 4.3.2 Prepositional Phrase Information

Original Text	Revised Version With Prepositional Phrase Removed
"I counted the keys in my hand" (Yang, 2018, p. 29).	I counted the keys.

Figure 4.3.3 Original Text vs. Revised Version With Prepositional Phrase Removed

Copyright material from Sean Ruday (2026), *Teaching Elementary Grammar with Mentor Texts*, Routledge

Reflection Question One	Reflection Question Two
How is the sentence different without the prepositional phrase "in my hand"?	Why do you think the author used this prepositional phrase?

Figure 4.3.4 Prepositional Phrase Reflection Questions Graphic Organizer

What Are Prepositional Phrases?	What Are Some Examples of Prepositional Phrases?	Why Are Prepositional Phrases Important to Strong Writing?	What Is a Published Example of Prepositional Phrase Use?
Prepositional phrases are descriptive phrases that begin with a preposition and end with a noun or pronoun called the object of the preposition.	On the chair Above the trees Under the desk Across the field	Prepositional phrases are important to strong writing because of the detail and description they add. This information can give the reader a clear understanding of what's being discussed.	"I counted the keys **in my hand**" (Yang, 2018, p. 29).

Figure 4.3.5 Prepositional Phrase Review Information

Copyright material from Sean Ruday (2026), *Teaching Elementary Grammar with Mentor Texts*, Routledge

Graphic Organizers from Lesson 4.4: Providing Detail: Relative Clauses

Relative Pronouns	Relative Adverbs
Who, Whose, Whom, Which, That	Where, When, Why

Figure 4.4.1 Relative Pronouns and Relative Adverbs

Grammatical Concept	What Are Relative Clauses?	What Are Examples of Relative Clauses?	How Can Relative Clauses Look in Writing?	Why Are Relative Clauses Important to Strong Writing?
Relative clauses	Relative clauses are grammatical tools that provide detail and description about nouns or pronouns and begin with relative pronouns or relative adverbs.	who loves the snow where the Boston Red Sox play which is her favorite sport	Liz, **who loves the snow**, is sledding. We visited Fenway Park, **where the Boston Red Sox play**. Tomorrow, Kim will play basketball, **which is her favorite sport**.	Relative clauses are important to strong writing because the detail and description they provide can enhance the reader's understanding of the noun or pronoun being discussed.

Figure 4.4.2 Relative Clause Information

Original Text	Revised Version With Relative Clause Removed
"I rub my cheek, which is creased from the ridges on the seat" (Rhodes, 2016, p. 12).	I rub my cheek.

Figure 4.4.3 Original Text vs. Revised Version With Relative Clause Removed

Copyright material from Sean Ruday (2026), *Teaching Elementary Grammar with Mentor Texts*, Routledge

Reflection Question One	Reflection Question Two
How is the sentence different without the relative clause "which is created from the ridges on the seat"?	Why do you think the author used this relative clause?

Figure 4.4.4 Relative Clause Reflection Question Graphic Organizer

What Are Relative Clauses?	What Are Some Examples of Relative Clauses?	Why Are Relative Clauses Important to Strong Writing?	What Is a Published Example of Relative Clause Use?
Relative clauses are grammatical tools that provide detail and description about nouns or pronouns and begin with relative pronouns or relative adverbs.	who loves the snow where the Boston Red Sox play which is her favorite sport	Relative clauses are important to strong writing because the detail and description they provide can enhance the reader's understanding of the noun or pronoun being discussed.	"I rub my cheek, **which is creased from the ridges on the seat**" (Rhodes, 2016, p. 12).

Figure 4.4.5 Relative Clause Review Information

Copyright material from Sean Ruday (2026), *Teaching Elementary Grammar with Mentor Texts*, Routledge

Graphic Organizers from Lesson 4.5: Clear and Powerful Language: Strong Verbs and Specific Nouns

Grammatical Concepts	What Are Strong Verbs and Specific Nouns?	What Are Examples of Strong Verbs and Specific Nouns?	How Can Strong Verbs and Specific Nouns Look in Writing?	Why Are Strong Verbs and Specific Nouns Important to Strong Writing?
Strong verbs and specific nouns	Strong verbs are verbs that clearly show exactly how an action was performed. **Specific nouns** are nouns that clearly indicate the person, place, thing, or idea being described.	Strong verb examples: Sprinted Whispered **Specific noun examples:** Pizza Restaurant	Strong verb examples in writing: I **sprinted** down the street. He **whispered** the information. **Specific noun examples in writing:** We smelled **pizza** as we entered the **restaurant**.	Strong verbs and specific nouns are important to strong writing because they communicate information clearly and help the reader understand what the writer is discussing.

Figure 4.5.1 Strong Verb and Specific Noun Information

Copyright material from Sean Ruday (2026), *Teaching Elementary Grammar with Mentor Texts*, Routledge

Original Text	Revised Version With Strong Verb Replaced by a Weaker Verb	Reflection Question
"Paloma **glanced** at the black cat and monkey in the painting" (Cervantes, 2019, p. 10).	Paloma **looked** at the black cat and monkey in the painting.	**Question:** Why do you think the strong verb "glanced" is important to the original text? **Our responses:**

Figure 4.5.2 Strong Verb Mentor Text Analysis Graphic Organizer

Original Text	Revised Version With Specific Noun Replaced by a More General Noun	Reflection Question
"This infected **mosquito** might bite you" (Kadohata, 2014, p. 2).	This infected **insect** might bite you.	**Question:** Why do you think the specific noun "mosquito" is important to the original text? **Our responses:**

Figure 4.5.3 Specific Noun Mentor Text Analysis Graphic Organizer

SUPPORT MATERIAL

What Are Strong Verbs and Specific Nouns?	What Are Examples of Strong Verbs and Specific Nouns?	Why Are Strong Verbs and Specific Nouns Important to Strong Writing?	What Are Published Examples of Strong Verbs and Specific Nouns?
Strong verbs are verbs that clearly show exactly how an action was performed. **Specific nouns** are nouns that clearly indicate the person, place, thing, or idea being described.	Strong verb examples: Sprinted Whispered Specific noun examples: Pizza Restaurant	Strong verbs and specific nouns are important to strong writing because they communicate information clearly and help the reader understand what the writer is discussing.	Published strong verb example: "Paloma **glanced** at the black cat and monkey in the painting" (Cervantes, 2019, p. 10). Published specific noun example: "This infected **mosquito** might bite you" (Kadohata, 2014, p. 2).

Figure 4.5.4 Strong Verb and Specific Noun Review Information

Graphic Organizers from Lesson 5.1: Linking and Connecting: Conjunctions

Conjunction Type	What It Is	Examples	Used in a Sentence
Coordinating conjunction	A word that connects related statements of equal importance.	for, and, nor, but, or, yet, so	Brody cooked the hamburgers, **and** Sawyer made the salad.
Correlative conjunction	A two-part structure that connects related statements of equal importance.	both-and, not only-but also, either-or, neither-nor	**Either** we will watch the movie today, **or** we will watch it tomorrow.
Subordinating conjunction	A word or phrase that connects two statements when one statement is dependent on the other.	after, although, because, before, if, since, until, while	**Since** the ground is covered with snow, we will go sledding.

Figure 5.1.1 Coordinating, Correlative, and Subordinating Conjunction Information

Copyright material from Sean Ruday (2026), *Teaching Elementary Grammar with Mentor Texts*, Routledge

Published Coordinating Conjunction Example	Published Correlative Conjunction Example	Published Subordinating Conjunction Example
"My voice catches in my throat, **and** I stumble over my words" (Keller, 2020, p. 6). From *When You Trap a Tiger* by Tae Keller	"You **either** like someone **or** you don't" (Medina, 2018, p. 126). From *Merci Suárez Changes Gears* by Meg Medina	"**Since** my mom and stepdad thought it was gross, we usually only got those toppings on half a pie" (Marks, 2020, p. 5). From *From the Desk of Zoe Washington* by Janae Marks

Figure 5.1.2 Published Coordinating, Correlative, and Subordinating Conjunction Examples

Coordinating Conjunction Mentor Text	Importance of the Coordinating Conjunction to the Sentence
"My voice catches in my throat, **and** I stumble over my words" (Keller, 2020, p. 6).	

Figure 5.1.3 Coordinating Conjunction Analysis Chart

Correlative Conjunction Mentor Text	Importance of the Correlative Conjunction to the Sentence
"You **either** like someone **or** you don't" (Medina, 2018, p. 126).	

Figure 5.1.4 Correlative Conjunction Analysis Chart

Copyright material from Sean Ruday (2026), *Teaching Elementary Grammar with Mentor Texts*, Routledge

Subordinating Conjunction Mentor Text	Importance of the Subordinating Conjunction to the Sentence
"**Since** my mom and stepdad thought it was gross, we usually only got those toppings on half a pie" (Marks, 2020, p. 5).	

Figure 5.1.5 Subordinating Conjunction Analysis Chart

Graphic Organizers from Lesson 5.2: Showing Emotion: Interjections

Grammatical Concept	What Are Interjections?	What Are Some Examples of Interjections	What Are Some Ways Interjections Can Look in Writing?	Why Are Interjections Important to Strong Writing?
Interjections	Interjections are single words or short phrases that writers use to show emotion.	Some examples of single-word interjections: wow, yay, ouch Some examples of short-phrase interjections: my gosh, no way, oh my	**Wow**, that was a great game. **Yay**! We're having pizza for dinner! **My gosh**, that's a heavy suitcase. **Oh my**! It snowed a lot last night.	Interjections are important to strong writing because they can help a writer or character show the emotion they're feeling, which can enhance the reader's understanding of the piece.

Figure 5.2.1 Interjection Information

Copyright material from Sean Ruday (2026), *Teaching Elementary Grammar with Mentor Texts*, Routledge

Original Text	Revised Version With Interjection Removed
"*Sweet!* That's when my braces come off!" (Winston, 2023, p. 6).	That's when my braces come off!

Figure 5.2.2 Original Text vs. Revised Version With Interjection Removed

Reflection Question One	Reflection Question Two
How is the sentence different without the interjection "Sweet!"?	Why do you think the author used this interjection in the text?

Figure 5.2.3 Interjection Reflection Questions Graphic Organizer

What Are Interjections?	What Are Some Examples of Interjections?	Why Are Interjections Important to Strong Writing?	What Is a Published Example of Interjection Use?
Interjections are single words or short phrases that writers use to show emotion.	Some examples of single-word interjections: wow, yay, ouch Some examples of short-phrase interjections: my gosh, no way, oh my	Interjections are important to strong writing because they can help a writer or character show the emotion they're feeling, which can enhance the reader's understanding of the piece.	"*Sweet!* That's when my braces come off!" (Winston, 2023, p. 6).

Figure 5.2.4 Interjection Review Information

Copyright material from Sean Ruday (2026), *Teaching Elementary Grammar with Mentor Texts*, Routledge

Graphic Organizers from Lesson 5.3: Pronouns and Clarity: Pronoun-Antecedent Agreement

Grammatical Concept	What Is Pronoun-Antecedent Agreement?	What Is an Example of Pronoun-Antecedent Agreement?	Why Is Pronoun-Antecedent Agreement Important to Strong Writing?
Pronoun-antecedent agreement	Pronoun-antecedent agreement is when pronouns clearly refer to the nouns they represent by matching in number, person, and gender as relevant to a statement.	The dogs wanted to rest, so they sat down in the yard. Note: In this sentence, the pronoun "they" agrees with the antecedent "the dogs" in number and in person.	Pronoun-antecedent agreement is important to strong writing because it helps readers clearly understand what the writer is trying to express. If a piece of writing has problems with pronoun-antecedent agreement, readers could be distracted by those problems or misunderstand the information in the piece.

Figure 5.3.1 Pronoun-Antecedent Agreement Information

Original Text	Revised Version Without Pronoun-Antecedent Agreement
"I watched him fold his jean jacket and put **it** in his duffel bag" (Wan-Long Shang, 2015, p. 35).	I watched him fold his jean jacket and put **them** in his duffel bag.

Figure 5.3.2 Original Text vs. Revised Version Without Pronoun-Antecedent Agreement

Reflection Question One	Reflection Question Two
How is the sentence different without pronoun-antecedent agreement?	Why is the pronoun-antecedent agreement important to the effectiveness of the original sentence?

Figure 5.3.3 Pronoun-Antecedent Agreement Reflection Question Graphic Organizer

What Is Pronoun-Antecedent Agreement?	Why Is Pronoun-Antecedent Agreement Important to Strong Writing?	What Is a Published Example of Pronoun-Antecedent Agreement?	Why Is Pronoun-Antecedent Agreement Present in This Example?
Pronoun-antecedent agreement is when pronouns clearly refer to the nouns they represent by matching in number, person, and gender as relevant to a statement.	Pronoun-antecedent agreement is important to strong writing because it helps readers clearly understand what the writer is trying to express. If a piece of writing has problems with pronoun-antecedent agreement, readers could be distracted by those problems or misunderstand the information in the piece.	"I watched him fold his jean jacket and put **it** in his duffel bag" (Wan-Long Shang, 2015, p. 35).	In this example, the pronoun "it" and the antecedent "jean jacket" agree in number and person: "it" is a singular, third-person pronoun that refers to the singular, third-person antecedent "jean jacket."

Figure 5.3.4 Pronoun-Antecedent Agreement Review Information

Copyright material from Sean Ruday (2026), *Teaching Elementary Grammar with Mentor Texts*, Routledge

Graphic Organizers from Lesson 5.4: Beyond the Literal: Figurative Language

Type of Figurative Language	Definition	Example
Similes	Similes are comparisons of two different things using the words *like* or *as*.	She ran to her dog like a race car speeding to the finish line.
Metaphors	Metaphors are comparisons of two different things that state one thing is another.	The cup of warm, delicious soup is a big hug.
Personification	Personification is the giving of human qualities to a nonliving thing.	The beach was calling to her.

Figure 5.4.1 Information About Similes, Metaphors, and Personification

Grammatical Concept	What Is Figurative Language?	What Are Some Types of Figurative Language?	Why Is Figurative Language Important to Strong Writing?
Figurative language	Figurative language is language that is not meant to be understood literally and provides description, emphasis, or expression to a piece of writing.	Some types of figurative language are similes, metaphors, and personification.	Figurative language is important to strong writing because it enhances the reader's understanding of what is being described and allows the author or character to express information in a way that is unique and memorable.

Figure 5.4.2 Figurative Language Information

Simile Mentor Text	Metaphor Mentor Text	Personification Mentor Text
"She ran like a kite that had been let loose on a gusty day, gliding across the sky, not stopping until it reached a tree" (Holt, 2023, p. 5). From *The Hurricane Girls* by Kimberly Willis Holt	"…the ocean is a strong woman…" (Mendez, 2023, p. 9). From *Aniana del Mar Jumps In* by Jasminne Mendez	"The sun shrugs over the edge of the globe…" (Schmidt, 2023, p. 5). From *The Labors of Hercules Beal* by Gary D. Schmidt

Figure 5.4.3 Figurative Language Mentor Texts

Original Text	Text Rewritten Without Simile	Reflection Question: Why Is the Simile Important to the Original Example?
"She ran like a kite that had been let loose on a gusty day, gliding across the sky, not stopping until it reached a tree" (Holt, 2023, p. 5).	She ran effortlessly.	

Figure 5.4.4 Simile Analysis Graphic Organizer

Copyright material from Sean Ruday (2026), *Teaching Elementary Grammar with Mentor Texts*, Routledge

Original Text	Text Rewritten Without Metaphor	Reflection Question: Why Is the Metaphor Important to the Original Example?
"…the ocean is a strong woman…" (Mendez, 2023, p. 9).	The ocean is powerful.	

Figure 5.4.5 Metaphor Analysis Graphic Organizer

Original Text	Text Rewritten Without Personification	Reflection Question: Why Is Personification Important to the Original Example?
"The sun shrugs over the edge of the globe…" (Schmidt, 2023, p. 5).	The sun moves over the edge of the globe.	

Figure 5.4.6 Personification Analysis Graphic Organizer

Copyright material from Sean Ruday (2026), *Teaching Elementary Grammar with Mentor Texts*, Routledge

What Is Figurative Language?	Why Are Some Types of Figurative Language?	Why Is Figurative Language Important to Strong Writing?	What Are Some Published Examples of Figurative Language?
Figurative language is language that is not meant to be understood literally and provides description, emphasis, or expression to a piece of writing.	Some types of figurative language are similes, metaphors, and personification.	Figurative language is important to strong writing because it enhances the reader's understanding of what is being described and allows the author or character to express information in a way that is unique and memorable.	Published simile example: "She ran like a kite that had been let loose on a gusty day, gliding across the sky, not stopping until it reached a tree" (Holt, 2023, p. 5). Published metaphor example: "…the ocean is a strong woman…" (Mendez, 2023, p. 9). Published personification example: "The sun shrugs over the edge of the globe…" (Schmidt, 2023, p. 5).

Figure 5.4.7 Figurative Language Review Information

Graphic Organizers from Lesson 5.5: Toward Clarity: Using Commas for Clarity

Type of Comma Use	Description	Example
Using commas to separate items in a series of three or more	Writers use commas to separate the items in a list when listing a series of three or more elements Note: The comma that comes before the word "and" in a series and before the final item in the series is optional unless otherwise stated by a specific writing style guide. I recommend using it for clarity and consistency. This comma is often called the serial comma or Oxford comma.	She loves basketball, hockey, and softball.

Figure 5.5.1 Comma Use Information

(Continued)

Type of Comma Use	Description	Example
Using commas to separate an introductory element from the rest of a sentence	Writers use commas to separate introductory elements from the rest of the sentence. An introductory element begins the sentence and provides background information or context but is not necessary for the sentence to function.	Because the weather is windy and rainy, we moved the party indoors.
Using commas to show direct address	Writers use commas to show someone is being directly addressed. The name or title of whoever is directly addressed is set off by a comma.	Newton, you are a wonderful dog.

Figure 5.5.1 (Continued)

Grammatical Concept	What Does It Mean?	What Are Some Types of It?	Why Is It Important to Strong Writing?
Using commas to make a piece of writing as clear as possible	Commas can make writing clear by separating pieces of information and showing the reader that one part of a sentence is set apart from another.	Some ways writers can use commas to make writing clear are: Using commas to separate items in a series of three or more Using commas to separate an introductory element from the rest of a sentence Using commas to show direct address	This grammatical concept is important to strong writing because it helps readers clearly understand the information in a piece of writing. If writers did not use commas to separate information, readers could be confused or could misunderstand the piece.

Figure 5.5.2 Information About Using Commas for Clarity

Copyright material from Sean Ruday (2026), *Teaching Elementary Grammar with Mentor Texts*, Routledge

Mentor Text: Using Commas to Separate Items in a Series of Three or More	Mentor Text: Using Commas to Separate an Introductory Element from the Rest of a Sentence	Mentor Text: Using Commas to Show Direct Address
"Mr. Hindley was manager, owner, and staff" (Kelly, 2020, p. 2). From *We Dream of Space* by Erin Entrada Kelly	"While I was searching, I found a headband I used to wear all the time when I was younger" (Patrick, 2020, p. 12). From *Tornado Brain* by Cat Patrick	"You gotta *fling* it, Genie" (Reynolds, 2017, p. 3). From *As Brave As You* by Jason Reynolds

Figure 5.5.3 Mentor Texts—Using Commas for Clarity

Original Text	Text Rewritten Without Commas That Separate Items in a Series of Three or More	Reflection Question: Why Are the Commas That Separate Items in the Series Important to the Original Example?
"Mr. Hindley was manager, owner, and staff" (Kelly, 2020, p. 2).	Mr. Hindley was manager owner and staff.	

Figure 5.5.4 Analysis—Using Commas to Separate Items in a Series of Three or More

Copyright material from Sean Ruday (2026), *Teaching Elementary Grammar with Mentor Texts*, Routledge

Original Text	Text Rewritten Without the Comma That Separates the Introductory Element from the Rest of the Sentence	Reflection Question: Why Is the Comma That Separates the Introductory Element from the Rest of the Sentence Important to the Original Example?
"While I was searching, I found a headband I used to wear all the time when I was younger" (Patrick, 2020, p. 12).	While I was searching I found a headband I used to wear all the time when I was younger.	

Figure 5.5.5 Analysis—Using Commas to Separate an Introductory Element from the Rest of a Sentence

Original Text	Text Rewritten Without the Comma That Shows Direct Address	Reflection Question: Why Is the Comma That Shows Direct Address Important to the Original Example?
"You gotta *fling* it, Genie" (Reynolds, 2017, p. 3).	You gotta *fling* it Genie.	

Figure 5.5.6 Analysis—Using Commas to Show Direct Address

Appendix C
Lesson Plan Template

This lesson plan template provides a way to use the lesson plan structure depicted in this book with additional grammatical concepts, mentor texts, and examples. You can use this planning template to follow this book's lesson plan format with your own mentor texts and examples. It can be especially useful when applying this book's approach to additional grammatical concepts.

Overview

(In this section, you'll share basic information about the lesson's focus, its sequence, and its key instructional activities)

Objectives

(In this section, you'll list key objectives for the instructional process):
-
-
-

Time Frame

(Here, you'll identify the time frame for the lesson sequence. The lessons in this book all take two class periods)

Copyright material from Sean Ruday (2026), *Teaching Elementary Grammar with Mentor Texts*, Routledge

Background Knowledge Required

(Here, you'll identify any background knowledge students need before beginning the lesson)

Materials Needed

(You'll list any materials you and your students need for the lesson):
-
-
-
-

Detailed Plan

Day One
1. Introduction
(You'll describe how you'll introduce the lesson. I recommend identifying the day's key questions and agenda items here)

2. Mini-Lesson
(You'll conduct a mini-lesson that describes key features of the grammatical concept on which you're focusing and discusses its importance)

3. Mentor Text Example
(You'll provide students with a published example of the focal grammatical concept)

4. Mentor Text Discussion and Analysis Activities
(You'll guide students through a discussion of the mentor text and related activities designed to help them understand the importance of the focal concept to the mentor text)

5. Exit Question
(You'll ask students to answer an exit question about the work they did that day on the focal concept)

Day Two
1. Introduction
(You'll share with students how the work they'll do that day builds on the previous lesson, provide the day's focal questions, and discuss the class period's agenda)

2. Review
(Here, you'll review key ideas, examples, and information you discussed with students the previous day)

3. Writing Activity
(In this activity, students apply the focal grammatical concept to their writing)

4. Reflection
(Here, students return to the passage they wrote and reflect on the importance of the focal grammatical concept to the passage)

5. Exit Question
(Students now answer a final exit question about the grammatical concept they worked on in this lesson)

Differentiation Ideas

(Here, you'll list possible ways to differentiate this lesson)
-
-
-
-

Assessment

(You'll identify ways you'll assess students' work in this instructional process)

Notes

- What worked when teaching this lesson?

- What might you adapt or change the next time you teach it?

For Product Safety Concerns and Information please contact our EU
representative GPSR@taylorandfrancis.com
Taylor & Francis Verlag GmbH, Kaufingerstraße 24, 80331 München, Germany

www.ingramcontent.com/pod-product-compliance
Lightning Source LLC
Chambersburg PA
CBHW081146230426
43664CB00018B/2821